THE INFRASTRUCTURE FINANCE CHALLENGE

The Infrastructure Finance Challenge

A Report by the Working Group on Infrastructure Finance, Stern School of Business, New York University

chaired by Professor Ingo Walter

NYU | STERN

NYU GLOBAL INSTITUTE FOR ADVANCED STUDY

OpenBook Publishers

https://www.openbookpublishers.com

Updated digital material and resources associated with this volume are available at https://www.openbookpublishers.com/isbn/9781783742936#resources

This is the third volume of our Open Reports Series.

ISSN (print): 2399-6668
ISSN (digital): 2399-6676

ISBN Paperback: 978-1-78374-293-6
ISBN Hardback: 978-1-78374-294-3
ISBN Digital (PDF): 978-1-78374-295-0
ISBN Digital ebook (epub): 978-1-78374-296-7
ISBN Digital ebook (mobi): 978-1-78374-297-4
DOI: 10.11647/OBP.0106

Cover image: Chi King, 'Glass and Steel (HONG KONG/ARCHITECTURE) IX' (2006), CC BY 2.0. Image from Wikimedia, https://commons.wikimedia.org/wiki/File:Glass_and_Steel_(HONG_KONG-ARCHITECTURE)_IX_(1426664677).jpg

All paper used by Open Book Publishers is SFI (Sustainable Forestry Initiative), PEFC (Programme for the Endorsement of Forest Certification Schemes) and Forest Stewardship Council(r)(FSC(r) certified.

Printed in the United Kingdom, United States and Australia
by Lightning Source for Open Book Publishers (Cambridge, UK).

Contents

Preface

The New York University Global Institute for Advanced Study is very pleased to support this important work on global infrastructure finance, led by Prof Ingo Walter of NYU's Stern School of Business.

The global interconnectedness of the world's economies, along with the torrid pace of urbanization in the developing world, lead to urgent and manifestly complex issues about infrastructure. This monograph takes on some of the fundamental questions in this area, attempting to clarify how to think about the boundaries of what is meant by 'infrastructure', its pricing, its potential adverse effects and its financing.

This monograph represents the first stage in what we expect to be a multi-year, multi-disciplinary exploration of these questions, so crucial to the future well-being of the developing world and, by extension, to that of the rest of the globe.

Initial work on the project includes participation in infrastructure financing panels discussions in the US, Europe and Asia, as well as a case study on the capital-market financing of a major Latin American urban highway project. Several additional case studies are underway which will lead to a case series available for use in university infrastructure courses around the world. A graduate-level infrastructure finance course at NYU Stern is being designed for launch in the fall of 2017. Research activity is focused on assembly of infrastructure financing datasets as well as an initial policy paper on infrastructure banks and their implications for the US. A steering committee will identify and launch additional research projects.

I am grateful to Prof Walter for his hard work on this project and to Dean Peter Henry for bringing the project to the attention of the GIAS.

Paul Boghossian
Director, Global Institute for Advanced Study
Julius Silver Professor of Philosophy
NYU

Executive Summary

Infrastructure and its effects on economic growth, social welfare, and sustainability receive a great deal of attention today. There is widespread agreement that infrastructure is a key dimension of global development and that its impact reaches deep into the broader economy, with important and complex implications for social progress.

There is equally broad agreement that infrastructure's dynamics are often hard to gauge. The external costs and benefits of infrastructure projects often differ materially from their internal costs and benefits. There are usually winners and losers, so in the political arena debates on infrastructure tend to be amplified. Consequently, infrastructure is a rich field for the kind of inquiry needed to craft sensible business strategies and public policies. They begin with the basics:

- Just what is "infrastructure", and where do its boundaries lie?

- How should infrastructure services be priced when they generate significant public goods whose benefits are hard to allocate?

- How should adverse effects of infrastructure projects be incorporated into their cost structures, to be passed forward to end-users and backward to investors?

- On the spectrum between private and public ownership, where should individual infrastructure projects fall? What is the appropriate role for public-private partnerships, purpose-specific infrastructure authorities, and build-operate-transfer models?

- What kinds of regulatory arrangements covering infrastructure projects are appropriate given widely differing political and economic circumstances?

- How should infrastructure development be financed, either on or off the public accounts of governments or private-sector sponsors? Where in the global pool of investable financial assets can infrastructure debt and equity best be placed?

This study focuses on the last of these issues — infrastructure finance. The scale of infrastructure investment needed in both developed and developing countries parallels the need for investable assets to create efficient portfolios in pension funds and other long-term managed asset pools. So a sustainable global equilibrium based on returns, costs, and risks can generate dramatic shared gains.

Some Key Conclusions

Infrastructure finance is among the most complex and challenging areas in the global financial architecture, and so the problem of assembling a set of sensible guideposts for it is equally formidable. We begin with a dozen findings backed by serious theoretical and empirical research:

1. Infrastructure development matters in the context of economic performance and growth.

2. Infrastructure tends to generate significant positive spillovers, and is therefore hard to price.

3. Infrastructure projects are usually large and complex, involving financial engineering that reflects their complexity and the need to align differing participant interests in pursuit of common gain.

4. Infrastructure projects usually extend over long periods of time, with their successive phases reflected in their capital structures

5. Risks surrounding infrastructure projects reflect their inherent complexity, ranging from cost overruns and delays to changes in government policies and *force majeure*.

6. The interaction between project complexity and risk can lead to highly contract-intensive financing arrangements. In turn, infrastructure finance in projects involving the private sector can combine equity, commercial loans, and fixed-income securities which must be taken up by suppliers of capital.

7. Commercial lending's role remains critical in the early phases of infrastructure project development, and is the province of financial intermediaries that have accumulated the necessary expertise (today predominantly European and Japanese banks).

8. The 2007–2008 global financial crisis — and the ensuing regulatory response focusing on risk-weighted assets, capital adequacy, liquidity, and funding stability in large financial institutions — do not seem to have materially impaired the availability of bank financing for viable infrastructure projects.

9. Efforts to tap global bond markets for infrastructure finance remain a work in progress in light of their risk ratings, maturities, and secondary market liquidity. Nevertheless, large asset managers have the opportunity to build expertise and appetite in this asset class, which would broaden this channel for infrastructure finance.

10. Based on the available evidence, infrastructure equity has performed well over various time periods, compared to the standard equity indexes and sector indexes such as commercial real estate.

11. An array of institutional initiatives and policy measures — including reforms in traditional multilateral agencies and new entrants — could be catalytic in addressing blockages in global infrastructure finance.

12. In the contemporary market environment, the overriding problem is less the shortage of available financing than the shortage of financeable infrastructure projects worldwide. This has retarded the migration of infrastructure finance from the public sector to global capital markets.

In this study, we explore each of these findings based on what we think we know about infrastructure finance and, where available, empirical evidence. It is structured in two parts: First, we review the key attributes and drivers of infrastructure development. Second, we examine the specifics of infrastructure financing.

1. Infrastructure, Performance and Economic Growth

To begin, we explore how infrastructure investments are, or should be, defined in a way that makes sense in the context of the world's complex and dynamic capital markets. They must be clearly-defined and operationally viable in order to be financeable in the real world of performance-driven asset portfolios.

Legal issues are always an important consideration in infrastructure finance, including ownership and governance of projects, questions of eminent domain, and regulation of infrastructure projects in private (or joint public/private) control. Labor relations, health and safety, and other social concerns are also critical. So are environmental impacts and sustainable development.[1] Here the public-goods characteristics of infrastructure often complicate the assessment of their benefits and costs in the real world of political economy. This raises the need for market discipline in the execution of infrastructure projects.

It is impossible to escape the drumbeat of commentary by media pundits, business experts, and government officials about the world's enormous infrastructure "needs" in the years ahead.

---

1   For example, the recent agreement by world leaders on transitioning to a low-carbon economy, together with the consensus on the UN Sustainable Development Goals (several of which relate directly to infrastructure needs), focuses attention on building green infrastructure and reducing the environmental footprint of existing infrastructure. In addition, infrastructure will need to be made climate resilient — that is, able to adapt to changing weather patterns.

In the US, for example, the American Society of Civil Engineers (ASCE) in 2015 awarded the country a minimally passing grade of D+ for its "crumbling" infrastructure. Attempting to estimate the opportunity cost of the most glaring deficiencies in terms of lost income, output, and growth, the ASCE identified some $3.6 trillion of unfunded infrastructure investment needed to remediate them. Other countries are said to be in better or worse shape than the US. Combined with the infrastructure needs of the developing world, such estimates highlight the enormous potential for infrastructure development — and the accompanying financial challenges.

The consulting firm McKinsey & Co. has estimated that the world will need to spend an aggregate $57 trillion (at 2010 prices) between 2013 and 2030 to keep up with infrastructure needs, or roughly $3.2 trillion per year in real terms. This estimate suggests a GDP spending shortfall of 1% for the OECD countries from 2007 through 2012 (from 3.5% to 2.5%) resulting from infrastructure under-spending, further retarding already sluggish economic growth around the world.[2]

More positively, OECD estimates suggest that annual worldwide spending on infrastructure will remain robust, averaging $1.8 trillion to $1.9 trillion annually through 2030, an increase from an average of $1.6 trillion per year from 2000 through 2010.

The Brookings Institution issued a report assessing the global infrastructure investment need between 2015 and 2030 at around $90 trillion, or $5 trillion to $6 trillion per year [Brookings, 2015]. The reality of fiscal constraints — in Europe, the US, and many other countries — could translate into a materially larger private-sector role in overall infrastructure finance.

Some observers have highlighted the missed opportunity for infrastructure spending during a time of low growth, low construction costs, low inflation, and historically low interest rates in many countries. Others point to indecisiveness and inordinate delay (sometimes far exceeding the duration of World War II) of projects designed to plug fairly ordinary but nevertheless significant infrastructure gaps.

Whatever the numbers, people seem to broadly agree that infrastructure is a key dimension of economic and social development

---

2   *The Economist*, 29 August 2015.

worldwide. They also concur that its impact reaches deep into the global economy, with important and complex implications for economic and social progress. As well, there is consensus that infrastructure dynamics can be difficult to gauge, with external costs and benefits sometimes differing materially from the internal costs and benefits.

Countries have a broad range of growth experiences. Some grow very slowly or not at all. Others experience growth spurts and then either slow down or experience a crisis and subsequently regress. A few developing countries have experienced sustained periods (25 years or more) of high growth, 6% or 7% annually on average, sometimes more.

Poor or inconsistent economic performance has many causes. Among them are flawed governance and faulty choices of growth models — that is, models that either do not work or have some "self-limiting" characteristics in terms of duration. Interestingly, the successful cases have common features. They are predominantly open-economy models. For developing economies, such interaction with the global economy offers two advantages.

One is access to advanced-country technology and know-how, which can accelerate a shift in potential productivity when imported and adapted. An economy's knowledge and technology base, embedded in its people and institutions, primarily determines that economy's productivity. The principal means of enabling long-term growth comes from augmenting that base through investment and innovation.

Second, the global economy provides a large market for tradable goods and services. The global market's size permits specialization in a way that a domestic economy, particularly a developing one, does not because of its relatively lower incomes and limited demand. Specialization via comparative advantage allows rapid economic expansion even with limited human and physical capital.

What do successful developing countries do, or need to do, to take advantage of this accelerated growth potential? The short answer is that they need to invest in infrastructure to deepen their economy's capital. Based on the known cases of sustained high growth, overall investment rates of 25% to 30% of GDP are required to sustain GDP growth above 6% to 7%.

Investment in all cases is a mix of public- and private-sector capital formation. The data on public-sector capex are surprisingly weak and inconsistent, especially in light of its central role in sustaining growth and competitiveness. Based on experience in an array of countries, public investment specifically in infrastructure projects in the range of 5% to 7% of GDP seems necessary. Private-sector investment would then need to be about 20% to 25% of GDP for overall investment to reach a 6–7% sustainable growth range. Most developing countries and many advanced countries fall short of this target.

For developing countries specifically, the shortfall reflects several factors. Investment rates at these levels, to the extent they are financed domestically, are "expensive" in terms of forgone short-term consumption. In relatively poor countries, this tradeoff often tips in favor of present consumption at the expense of investment that would allow higher levels of future consumption. For understandable reasons, developing countries have a very high social discount rate that, in the reality of political economy, can overshadow the requisites of investment-generated growth.

In particular, private-sector domestic and cross-border investment can fall short for several reasons. It requires a secure investment environment, which means that property rights are reasonably respected and that factors affecting return on investment (e.g., taxation and regulation) are predictable and not subject to arbitrary change. This is a matter of commitment, confidence, and establishing a track record. Without a relatively secure investment environment, extraneous risk undermines investment and/or redirects it to more attractive venues in the global economy.

The tradable part of the world economy is very competitive, a fact that was underappreciated for many years. China's rise as a manufacturing source, with its very large scale and absorptive capacity, made policymakers much more aware of growth policy's competitive dynamics.

As noted, the core of attracting both domestic and international private capital lies with investment in complementary public tangible and intangible assets, primarily human capital and infrastructure. Augmenting these assets increases the return to private investment and leverages it on both the tradable and non-tradable sides of a national economy. The tradable side drives growth because of its enhanced capacity to expand rapidly. Rising incomes then generate increased demand on the non-tradable side.

Public-sector investment reflects how a developing country exploits its comparative advantage. Attractively priced and mobile human capital is key. The next important component comes from infrastructure that delivers power and telecommunications reliably, as well as ports, roads, rail links, and airports that, properly regulated, lower the cost of logistics and raise the return on investment in plant and equipment. In today's world of climate change and water scarcity, environmental infrastructure also has increasing importance.

Fifty years ago, this growth model's elements were not as well understood as they are today. Growth in the developing world was quite limited prior to World War II, so economists had very few examples for modeling the growth process. Because it is easily replicated, useful knowledge has a powerful capacity to spread growth making knowledge the basis of "catch-up" growth. But that fact was not well appreciated at the time. The complementarity of public and private investment was likewise underappreciated. People thought that a country could make the tradable part of the economy grow by excluding external competition (the import-substitution model) rather than by taking direct steps to drive up productivity.

Based on historical experience in developing countries, the role of investment (private and complementary public) is now reasonably well understood. And yet, patterns of underinvestment persist, particularly in infrastructure. High-investment cases are the exception rather than the rule. The question is, why?

To begin answering this question, we focus on how needed investment, particularly public-sector investment, is financed and by whom. In the exceptional cases of sustained high growth cited earlier, public-sector investment has been financed largely domestically. In contrast, numerous cases of substantial external financing of public investment (or external financing of the government in general) did not result in sustained high growth. Indeed, they often ended badly in economic slowdowns, crises, and defaults. So the history of using the global economy's capacity to invest in order to overcome the challenge of generating sufficient funding from domestic sources — including the government's capital budget — suggests that there are serious obstacles to doing so. In a nutshell, public-sector investment is the crucial ingredient in all known recipes for a country to achieve sustained patterns of inclusive growth. For the most part, however, external funding has not so far succeeded in this arena.

As noted earlier, domestic infrastructure funding requires a tradeoff between present and future consumption — a tradeoff that most lower-income countries have trouble making. Yet large pools of investable funds are eager to underwrite infrastructure if the risk and return parameters are suitable. And the social benefits, to the extent that they exceed the private returns to investors, are viewed as a plus by many institutional investors.

The propensity to underinvest in infrastructure is not confined to developing countries, where arguably the affordability and time-value of consumption issues are more dramatic. Why is that?

First, the importance to long-term growth of public investment in general, and infrastructure in particular, is not well understood.

Second, as with all issues involving tradeoffs of present consumption for future benefits and growth, the question of "who pays" invariably comes up. It is often referred to as the "burden-sharing" issue. In many economies, an inability to resolve this issue in what is generally agreed as a "fair" way causes inaction even when the problem is well diagnosed. "Fairness", after all, tends to be subjective.

Third, deficiencies in infrastructure investment produce no immediate negative effects, other than distorting the composition of aggregate demand. It takes a while before a bridge collapses, for instance. Deferred maintenance is a ubiquitous problem and not confined to the public sector. More generally, under financial pressure or with competing claims, all economic sectors defer expenditures that lack immediate negative consequences — including businesses, households, governments, and non-profits.

Fourth, there are good arguments for financing the investment component of public-sector expenditure with debt. Essentially, using debt rather than current tax revenues produces less tax distortion in resource allocation over the life of the assets and their social/economic benefits. In the present context, however, real and perceived constraints on public debt levels and ratios lead to underinvestment.

Finally, in this distinctly "second-best" set of conditions (unusually constrained at present), are there new funding models in which private, quasi-private, and external pools of capital can help fund investment in infrastructure? If so, what are they, and in what areas of infrastructure do they apply? Moreover, what obstacles must be removed to make them part of the solution? These questions provide our focus for this study.

A final word of caution: Underinvestment on the public-sector side of infrastructure development creates an important growth constraint. But it is not the only one. The absence of structural flexibility and mobility of resources is another, and major failures of inclusiveness in the labor force are a key factor. In addition, the return on public-sector investment in terms of elevated growth and future incomes depends on the presence or absence of complementary conditions and, if necessary, meaningful reforms.

2. Investable Infrastructure Assets

To economists, infrastructure is a type of durable capital not provided efficiently by the private market alone. Because the market generally does a reasonably good job of providing housing and commercial office buildings, these types of long-lived capital are typically not considered infrastructure. Specialized buildings used mainly by a government agency, however, are sometimes included in definitions of infrastructure.

Durable capital that provides infrastructure services is typically configured as a "network" in physical space. Examples include a system of roads, water conduits, sewer pipes, electrical transmission and communication lines. When network services are provided in an unregulated market, they tend toward monopoly because a larger network is relatively more efficient at delivering services than a smaller one. So there is almost always a role for some government entity in providing infrastructure services. For example, some types of network capital such as roads are mainly provided by government agencies. Others, such as telecoms or power grids, are often provided by regulated private firms.

The World Economic Forum (2014) has taken an expansive view, defining infrastructure as "the physical structures — roads, bridges, airports, electrical grids, schools, hospitals — that are essential for a society to function and an economy to operate".[1] This section partitions the infrastructure universe along several relevant dimensions. Table

---

1   World Economic Forum, *op. cit.* above.

1 presents one possible taxonomy by OECD in terms of the associated *sectors*.

Table 1. Key Infrastructure Sectors (Source: OECD, 2014)

Sectors	Examples
Power and energy	Energy productions, power distribution
Water and sewerage	Plants for management of the water cycle
Telecom	Satellite communication networks
Transportation	Highways, tunnels, bridges, light rails, ports/ harbours, airports
Social infrastructures	Social Housing, Hospitals, prisons, schools

Infrastructure encompasses a very broad set of asset types, and the line separating the free market from a regulated market or government provision differs among societies. Consequently, there is some divergence as to what sectors are included and excluded from infrastructure in various economies.

An example from data provider MSCI illustrates this point. MSCI constructs the World Core Infrastructure Index (WCII), the World Infrastructure Index (WII), and the Emerging Markets Infrastructure Index (EMII), three widely followed benchmark indexes of publicly listed infrastructure firms.

Table 2 presents the Global Industry Classification Standard (GICS) names of the constituent sectors, as well as each subsector's weight in the indexes on 6 May 2015.

The WCII and WII assign the largest weight to *Utilities* (with subsectors Electric, Gas, Water, and Multi-Utilities, as well as Oil & Gas Storage & Transportation). The WCII gives a large weight to *Transport Infrastructure*, while the other two indexes weight *Telecommunication Infrastructure* more heavily.

Wireless telecom is subject to much weaker local scale economies than services provided by a physical network. For example, it is much easier for several different wireless service providers to have customers in the same city block than for several water suppliers to do the same. One might argue that investments in a wireless network are more like commercial office buildings and should not count as infrastructure.

Nevertheless, wireless telecom holds a particularly prominent place in the EMII. The WCII excludes social infrastructure.

These differences in industry composition lead to substantial divergence in asset return performance and affect the optimal size of "infrastructure" as an asset class in institutional portfolios. Definitions matter, so we aim to be precise about our definition of infrastructure here.

Table 2. Infrastructure Sector and Subsector Weights (Source: MSCI, 2015)

GICS Sub-industry	WCII		WII		EMII	
Oil & Gas Storage & Transportation	16.7		10.5		2.5	
Electric Utilities	14.4		21.3		12.4	
Gas Utilities	11.1		2.9		4.7	
Water Utilities	4.1		1.1		2.3	
Multi-Utilities	13.9		15.4			
Utilities		60.2		51.1		21.9
Railroads	14.1					
Airport Services	3.6		0.8		2.8	
Highways & Rail tracks	10.4		1.6		2.5	
Marine Ports & Services	2.0		0.3		3.2	
Transport Infrastructure		30.2		2.71		8.46
Specialized REITs	9.6					
Alternative Carriers			1.1			
Integrated Telecommunication Services			32.4		15.8	
Wireless Telecommunication Services			10.8		47.5	
Telecommunications Infrastructure		9.6		44.3		63.2
Education Services			0.1			
Health Care Facilities			1.8		4.1	
Social Infrastructure		0.0		1.8		4.1
	100.0	100.0	100.0	100.0	97.7	97.7

RARE Infrastructure Limited (2013) estimates the total size of all global infrastructure assets in 2012 at $20 trillion. A division of infrastructure by *asset ownership* suggests that 75% is government owned and 25% is privately owned (see Figure 1).

The world investable market portfolio contains about $100 trillion in private assets, and non-governmental infrastructure assets represent 5% of the world market portfolio. Equity invested in publicly listed and unlisted funds represents approximately $3 trillion of this $5 trillion, with debt representing the remaining $2 trillion in private capital. Unlisted equity (direct investment) contributes about $450 billion, and this amount is likely to grow substantially. The number of unlisted funds investing in infrastructure tripled between 2007 and 2015. Pension funds and sovereign wealth funds have expressed strong interest in further expanding their infrastructure asset allocations.

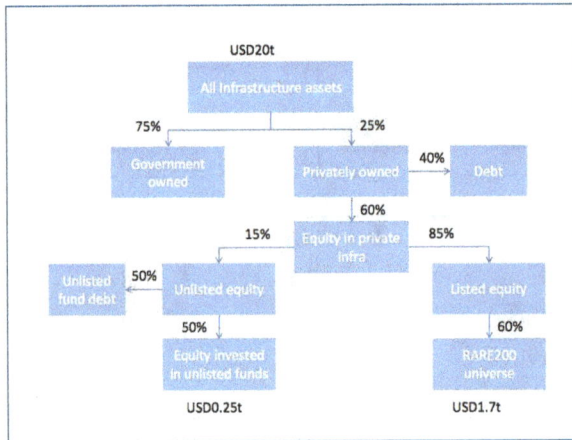

Figure 1. Infrastructure Participation (Source: World Bank, FactSet Research System, RARE calculations, Preqin)

Some infrastructure assets are for social use, such as prisons or educational or medical facilities, while others are for economic use, such as toll roads or airports. Some infrastructure services are used by a government agency to provide a final service, and others are provided directly to consumers and private firms. Many types of privately provided infrastructure (e.g., toll roads) come with demand guarantees from a government agency.

Figure 2 shows the spectrum of possible private involvement in infrastructure investment, listing the combinations of private and public ownership, use, and operations.

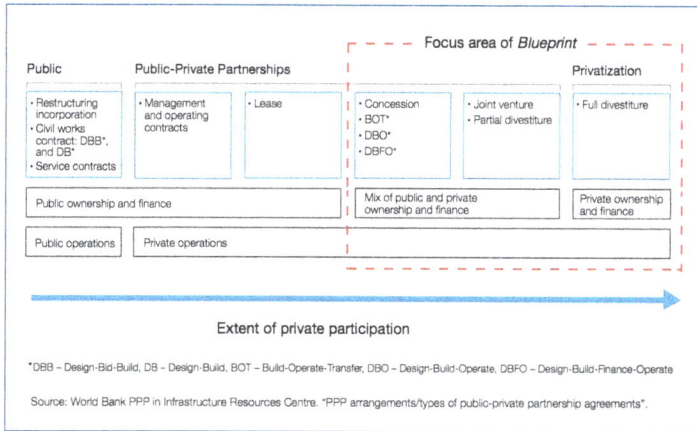

Figure 2. Extent of Private Participation

One can also divide the infrastructure universe by *asset stage* into "greenfield" and "brownfield". Greenfield projects involve constructing a new asset on previously undeveloped terrain, and they often generate little or no income in the near term. Brownfield projects redevelop an existing site for infrastructure purposes, converting it to a new use or expanding its existing use.

The *asset location* matters, but labels such as mature, maturing, and emerging markets are of questionable usefulness. More important are the location's political risk, regulatory risk, and management and governance risk (e.g., corruption). Under the definition suggested by economists, efficiently providing infrastructure requires an active role by some government entity. Infrastructure can therefore suffer from a government that is either too weak or too expansive.

Finally, the *nature of the income stream* is a crucial driver of risk and returns. Assets whereby the investor has a long-term contract or concession with a sovereign counterparty that delivers predictable (or even regulator-determined) revenues and costs represent one extreme of the spectrum. Assets with market-based revenue streams that have income volatility because of less reputable counterparties represent the other. Table 3 combines the various asset characteristics into an increasing risk-and-return profile ranging from mature infrastructure assets (low risk) to growth infrastructure assets (moderate risk) to development projects (high risk). The nature of the income risk and the mix of capital stake and fee structure determine whether the asset is more bond- or more stock-like. That in turn affects the relevant valuation framework.

Table 3. Asset Return and Risk Profiles (Source and © MSCI, 2014)

<table>
<tr><th colspan="2"></th><th colspan="3">INVESTMENT STYLE</th></tr>
<tr><th colspan="2"></th><th>Low Risk</th><th>Moderate Risk</th><th>High Risk</th></tr>
<tr><td rowspan="5">INVESTMENT FEATURES</td><td>Return driver</td><td>• **Income yield** is a significant component of total return target</td><td>• **Income & capital** contribute in generally equal proportion to total return</td><td>• **Capital return** drives total return over the short to medium term. Yield builds over time as capex sinks, revenues grow, & debt is refinanced</td></tr>
<tr><td>Income stream</td><td>• **Predictable, regulated** revenues & costs
• **Long-term** contract/ concession
• Sovereign counterparties (AAA or similar) pay revenues unrelated to volume/usage</td><td>• Relatively **predictable, stable** revenues & costs
• **Medium-term** contract
• Income streams with steady growth profile
• Strong operational focus</td><td>• **Market-based** revenue streams with some degree of income **volatility**
• Assets in **development stage** or **emerging** markets</td></tr>
<tr><td>Investment horizon</td><td>• **Long-term** investment horizon</td><td>• **Medium to long-term** investment horizon</td><td>• **Short to medium-term** investment horizon
• Characterised by J-curve investment phase</td></tr>
<tr><td>Market exposure</td><td>• Geographically **mature** markets</td><td>• Geographically **mature** markets
• Geographically **maturing** markets</td><td>• Geographically **mature** markets
• Geographically **maturing** markets
• Geographically **emerging** markets</td></tr>
<tr><td>Asset stage</td><td>• **Existing / brownfield** assets
• **Stabilized** income stream
• Relatively **low volatility**</td><td>• Existing & **rehabilitated brownfield** assets
• Government **privatisations**
• **Greenfield** assets (**social uses**)</td><td>• **High-risk brownfield** assets
• **Greenfield** assets (**economic uses**)</td></tr>
<tr><td rowspan="2">INVESTMENT FEATURES</td><td>Example</td><td>• **Social infrastructure operations**
• **Power & utilities** (transmission & distribution)
• **Water & waste** management systems
• Pipelines (long term contracts, regulated)
• Toll roads (established trunks with limited competition)</td><td>• **Power generation** (**long-term** contracts)
• **Toll roads** (established, but with **demand risks**)
• **Social infrastructure construction**
• **Airports & seaports** (**established hubs**)
• Pipelines (medium term contracts, unregulated)</td><td>• Pipelines - short term contracts, unregulated
• Merchant power plants
• Contracted power generation - short term contracts
• Greenfield toll roads</td></tr>
<tr><td>External factors</td><td>• **Transparent regulatory & legal** landscape
• Stable, **low volatility macroeconomic** history</td><td>• **Moderate political, macroeconomic, & contract risks**
• Additonal **development & project risks** associated with greenfield infrastructure</td><td>• **Opaque regulatory** regime
• **High political risk**
• **Subsidy dependent** industries
• Exposure to **technology risk, demand volatility, & pricing risk**</td></tr>
</table>

Source: IPD

3. Infrastructure Attributes and Problems of Market Failure

Based on the definitions in the preceding section, we consider "infrastructure" to encompass the following specific kinds of facilities:

- Transport: Roads, bridges, and tunnels; rail systems; airports and air traffic control; harbors and ports;

- Power and energy: Electrical generation units; high-voltage electrical distribution; refineries and natural and shale gas liquefaction and regasification units; natural gas and petroleum pipelines and distribution centers; and the newer entrants: renewable energy, battery storage, micro grids, and smart transport grids;

- Water and sewage: Canals and irrigation systems; water purification plants; water pipelines; sewage pipelines; sewage treatment systems; as well as green infrastructure such as wetlands, greening of impervious surfaces for storm-water capture, forest carbon sinks, and watershed protection, among others;

- Telecom: Landline telephone systems; landline cable and broadband systems; satellite networks; cell/mobile networks; and

- Social: Public housing; schools; hospitals; prisons.

Although green infrastructure represents a newer asset class, we nevertheless include it in our definition because of its exponential

© New York University/Stern School of Business, CC BY 4.0   http://dx.doi.org/10.11647/OBP.0106.03

growth that will be scaled in response to recent global policy commitments as well as by individual governments. China, for example, has developed an aggressive infrastructure plan that includes public- or private-sector financing aimed at tackling its problems with water availability and quality, air pollution and soil degradation.

As noted, scale economies, particularly those that operate in a concentrated geographical area, make it impossible for a competitive market to provide many infrastructure services. These "market failure" problems — competitive markets' inability to encompass the characteristics of infrastructure facilities; significant information asymmetries; and significant positive spillover effects — are related to some of these facilities' typical characteristics, as follows:[1]

- Significant economies of scale tend to exist in the facilities' construction and operation. Larger facilities are less costly on a per-unit-of-output basis than are otherwise similar but smaller facilities.

- Infrastructure facilities tend to be capital intensive, requiring a large amount of investment relative to their annual output and/or to the amount of labor needed for their operation. This capital intensity usually contributes to their economies of scale.

- The facilities tend to be long-lived and often last for generations, although many residential and commercial facilities share this characteristic.

- Most societies perceive infrastructure facilities as serving broad public goals. In some instances they may be true "public goods" for which the facility's positive externalities are pervasive. That is, additional individuals can receive benefits from the facilities at little or no incremental resource cost and without reducing others' benefits — and it is difficult or impossible to exclude anyone from receiving those benefits.[2]

---

1   We discuss several important exceptions in the following text.
2   A local mosquito eradication program is a clear example of a "public good" that meets these criteria; national defense is another frequently cited example.

In other instances, the facilities are simply seen as central to the basic functioning of a society. Still, many public goods (e.g., mosquito abatement) are clearly not infrastructure. Indeed, most infrastructure is a rival good, so technically they are "club goods", not public goods in the strict sense of the term.

It is worth exploring the connections between these core infrastructure characteristics and the problems they pose for competitive markets. First, however, two counterexamples help illustrate many of the points that need to be taken into account:

Consider roads and highways. Projects in this area have the characteristics that have just been described, and they are generally considered to be a part of "infrastructure". But what about the gasoline stations which service the vehicles that use roads and highways? At first glance, these stations are just as essential to transportation and should be considered as part of "infrastructure". Yet they are generally not included as such. Why not?

It seems highly likely that their exclusion from the infrastructure category is because gas stations are viable at a relatively small scale; they are not especially capital-intensive; they are not especially long-lived; and they do not have strong "public goods" features. In addition, the direct sale of their output — "pay as you go"— to consumers or end-users is considered a "natural" market arrangement. So the market-driven system can generally develop a near-optimum network of gas stations to accompany a road system, and gas stations thus are not considered to be part of "infrastructure" or part of the "infrastructure problem". As communication technology advances, the time will soon come when road-use tolling will allow "pay as you go" pricing for road use, and this issue may well disappear.

A second counterexample is worth considering: Electric power generation — primarily in the form of large-scale fossil fuel, nuclear, or hydro facilities — has traditionally demonstrated the foregoing characteristics and has been considered part of "infrastructure". A reason for natural monopoly is a minimum efficient scale for a plant that is large compared with the market. But power generation is a service whereby the minimum efficient scale for a plant appears to be decreasing relative to market demand in the immediate area it can service. So in this segment, we increasingly have an opportunity to separate the services provided by the grid from the services of individual generating plants.

Consequently, a market-based system of power generation units may become feasible. If low prices for natural gas persist, power generation facilities based on natural gas, tidal energy, wind, and solar may proliferate. In response, many of the grid-related infrastructure problems currently associated with electricity generation may diminish in importance.

What are the key connections between the characteristics of traditional infrastructure facilities and the problems that accompany them?

3.1 Economies of Scale

Cost efficiency often calls for larger-size infrastructure facilities. Consequently only one or a few facilities may be needed to serve a given market. When prices can be charged for an output, a single supplier of this output means a monopoly seller. Even if a few facilities can serve the market, oligopolistic behavior may interfere with a fully competitive process.

With monopoly (or coordinated oligopoly) come some important implications. Textbook microeconomics tells us that a monopoly will charge a higher price and sell less output than an otherwise similar competitive group of sellers. Without a competitive process to keep prices reasonably close to costs, society faces a set of choices regarding how the facility will be operated:

1. Society (collectively) "grits its teeth" and decides to allow a private-sector monopolist to operate unimpeded (unregulated with respect to price);

2. Society decides to allow a private-sector monopolist to sell the output, but places limits, through some form of regulation, on the price that the monopolist can charge; or

3. Society decides that the service will be provided by an arm of the state. In this case, a private-sector entity might build the

facility under some form of contracting with the government, or the government might build the facility itself.

Regardless of which route is selected, efficiency issues will arise. For the unregulated private-sector monopoly, a high price will mean that output is lower than it would be if the price were closer to costs. For the regulated private-sector monopoly, setting an appropriate regulated price — so that efficient costs are covered but the firm cannot take advantage of its market power or "gold plate" its costs — is rarely an easy task. For the government-operated facility, the pricing issue is equally relevant, but a challenge arises: How to keep operating costs efficient when the profit motive is not an inherent part of the process?

These efficiency questions become yet more difficult when a facility is complex and offers multiple services. For example, an airport is an intermediary between airlines and fliers. The airport can charge the airlines for takeoff/landing slots, gate facilities, and hangar/storage/repair facilities. For in-airport services such as parking, food, and travel-related paraphernalia, the airport can either charge fliers directly or charge the vendors that provide these services. Efficiency issues can arise with all of those services and the charges for them.

Another efficiency consequence of a single supplier is often overlooked but nevertheless important. Unlike in a competitive environment, where sellers offer a variety of qualities and attributes in response to consumers' differing preferences (e.g., the retail sale of clothing, food, automobiles, etc.), a single provider usually offers a single quality (or at most a limited range of qualities).

For example, in electricity distribution, different levels of reliability are possible with respect to service interruption (e.g., due to weather-related breaks in above-ground wires). A single provider, however, can provide only a single level of reliability, even if the various consumers within the customer base have differing preferences with respect to reliability levels — and consequently different willingness to pay the costs associated with achieving that reliability.

This unavoidable limitation on variety generally exists whenever there is a single provider, whether a private-sector entity or an arm of the government, and whether the facility is a true "public good" or perceived as central to the functioning of society.

3.2 Capital-intensity

An infrastructure facility's capital intensity describes the size of investments needed relative to output. The presence of economies of scale, for example, concentrates the large investments required for a single facility such as an airport or a single contiguous power grid.

Regardless of whether the public or private sector controls the facility, debt finance has historically been needed for a large share of such investments. The main issue is that when a government entity retains control of the facility, equity financing cannot include control rights. In turn, the need for debt finance raises a familiar set of asymmetric information problems with respect to financing arrangements. The borrower needs to provide assurances, both before and during the debt contract, that the lender will be repaid. The more difficult it is for the borrower to do so, the more risky the debt contract will appear to the lender, and the more costly this contract will be to the borrower. Under such conditions, the conventional creditor can only lose, never gain, although it is possible to create equity-like securities that bear more risk associated, for example, with fluctuations in demand.

3.3 Long-lived Immobile Assets

An infrastructure facility's typical long-lived nature increases the likelihood that its developer will seek long-term financing. But long-term finance itself exacerbates the financing problems just discussed. The longer a financial contract's term, the greater the possibility that circumstances could change in a way that makes it more difficult for the borrower to service the debt. Consequently long-term financing is generally perceived as more risky and usually is more costly than shorter-term financing.

3.4 Serving General Public Goals

If an infrastructure facility is perceived as serving broad public goals, then the political process will likely create pressures for low charges, possibly below levels that would cover costs. In addition, to the extent that significant (and likely) economies of scale exist, marginal costs will be below average costs until a capacity constraint is reached, or until the difficulties of managing a large facility kick-in. So, a good economic argument can be made for setting prices that are equal only to marginal costs and that thus do not cover fixed costs.

In either case, the issue of how to cover total costs becomes relevant and important. A similar question arises in the case of a pure "public good", for which prices cannot be charged because individuals for political or practical reasons cannot be excluded from enjoying the benefits of the facility's output.

In turn, these pricing issues affect financing for infrastructure facilities through creditors' perceived riskiness of the debt arrangements. This holds true whether the facility is operated by a private-sector entity (and subject to price regulation) or by a public-sector entity whereby the debt-related payments are linked to the cash flows generated by the facility. And for the pure public good, the political willingness of governmental entities to honor their debt obligations raises the same risk issues.

Consequently, infrastructure finance needs to have an explicit focus on public finance in general, more than the usual idea of a binary separation of tasks between a unified "government" and the market. It must also address the division of tasks between local and national public finance. If in this context there is a role for public borrowing, notably at the local level in federal or otherwise decentralized political systems, what will it take to make this market work better?

Most infrastructure projects require a physical network that extends through three-dimensional space. Because competition between different physical networks is nearly impossible, the government almost always plays a pivotal role in developing and operating infrastructure. One critical bottleneck that holds up investment in new infrastructure projects is assembling the necessary sites and easements, often by eminent domain. Especially in the case of urban infrastructure, big efficiency gains are available if the government takes the simple step of specifying a grid of public space to be used for trunk infrastructure before private investment takes place.

Different governments have different capacities and comparative advantages, so the state's specific role varies from country to country. This heterogeneity means that one important function of the global financial system may be to convert income streams from different countries into standardized securities that can be traded in liquid markets, as discussed below. The need for liquidity complements financial markets' more familiar functions such as diversifying idiosyncratic risks and resolving asymmetric information problems.

3.5 Sustainability

Investment in infrastructure has been central to achieving economic development goals, but with it has come a host of environmental and social challenges. For instance, the world's current on-line infrastructure facilities are responsible for roughly 50% of global greenhouse gas emissions. Infrastructure projects have destroyed ecosystems that protect against flooding (e.g., wetlands) or act as carbon sinks (e.g., forests). They have displaced native peoples, often leaving them in poverty. China's resource- and infrastructure-heavy growth has made 60% of its groundwater unfit for human consumption, generated air pollution at toxic levels over large swaths of the country and left 19% of its arable land too polluted for agricultural use.[3]

The country's aggressive "take no prisoners" approach to growth was sustainable only as long as the social benefits were seen to exceed the social costs. Even under one-party rule, political sustainability will eventually be called into question once a nation's material needs have been successfully addressed — unless those costs in the form of deforestation, overfishing, toxic mining spoil, species extinction etc. can be shifted to others. This is trans-frontier environmental degradation through trade and foreign investment. At least domestically, China has developed environmental targets and a public-private partnership investment framework to invest in retrofitting old infrastructure and develop new projects with fewer negative externalities.

This challenge is not confined to emerging economies, although most developed countries have had the means and the luxury of incorporating

---

3   Goldman Sachs Group, "China's Environment" July 15, 2015 at http://www. goldmansachs.com/our-thinking/pages/interconnected-markets-folder/chinas-environment/report.pdf

long-lasting, high-level sustainability safeguards for more than a half century. Still, neglect and delay along with budget constraints virtually guarantee that old legacies will re-emerge. For example, the 2016 water supply crisis in Flint, Michigan exposed residents to high levels of lead, pointing to underinvestment in environmental and health attributes of basic infrastructure services. Months after the issue arose, no resolution had been found regarding accountability or remediation responsibility.

On a global level, the UN Sustainable Development Goals (SDGs) include criteria on clean energy, infrastructure, sustainable cities, and climate action that will require a new 21st century approach to infrastructure. This new approach covers broad objectives, such as reducing carbon and other environmental impacts, as well as support for new technologies such as electric self-driving vehicles and transportation grids in urban centers.

"Green" costs money, however. In the years following the 2007–2009 financial crisis and the Great Recession, the need for project-related financing grew steadily. According to Brookings [2015], the incremental costs to "green" these investments and make them sustainable could be as much as $4 trillion in gross terms, not including operational savings and positive externalities. Perhaps in the end, the benefits significantly exceed the costs. But it is the costs that must be credibly defined and financed.

3.6 The Broader Implications

The brief overview contained in this section on the economics of infrastructure development offers some further implications that can be summarized as follows:

- Getting infrastructure "right" is a difficult analytical challenge because of issues about "scale" relative to market size.

- Government will always be involved in infrastructure projects. Because the capacity for governance and the sophistication of the supporting political process will vary across jurisdictions, different systems for providing infrastructure will be appropriate in different contexts.

- Sustainable and green infrastructure aimed at solving environmental and social challenges is a growing priority.

- Technological innovation is opening up many new options.

- Some types of service, such as power generation, that were previously infrastructure services may increasingly be provided in a competitive market.

- Demand exists for new types of infrastructure, such as a grid of fiber optic lines.

- New information technology could allow much more detailed monitoring of use as well as new categories of user fees based on these measures, which can address some of the free-rider problems in certain types of infrastructure.

Infrastructure financing issues in light of generic drivers are as real and substantial as the projects themselves. Although understanding the nature of these problems does not automatically eliminate them, improved understanding can point toward design and implementation strategies that may lessen their severity. The world's infrastructure needs are of such magnitude that even modest improvements in financial efficiency could create significant gains.

4. Legal Structures and Frameworks

Numerous legal and regulatory issues arise in infrastructure finance, often creating barriers to project development. The most important involves securing a grid of space that can support at least the trunk lines for any networked infrastructure. Other issues concern the clear definition of property rights and the enforcement of long-term contracts with constituencies such as customers and organized labor. A diverse range of social concerns also arises, such as privacy for communications network users or safety for residents who live near nuclear power plants.

As discussed earlier with respect to environmental sustainability, non-economic issues are usually reflected in regulation of infrastructure projects. Such issues have become prominent and seem likely to grow further in influence. They help drive not only the sources of financing but also the key risk profiles of projects through completion, operation, and market or off-take conditions.

4.1 Land as a Key Issue in Network Infrastructure

Because a landowner holds a monopoly regarding the land's use in a grid that passes through the property, neither a government nor a private party that wants to acquire land for grid-based infrastructure can rely on purchases in a competitive market.

In places where private individuals have extensive property rights to land, eminent domain offers a mechanism for acquiring land that is not subject to unlimited monopoly distortions. In places where individuals lack such *de jure* rights, they may still have *de facto* rights that present the same impediment to the construction of a new network, and a process analogous to eminent domain may still be necessary. Even in places where the government retains both legal and *de facto* rights over key uses of land, some compensation system may still be required when a government exercises its right to build a network on specific parcels.

Any such process will be easier to implement if private individuals have not yet made large, site-specific durable capital investments on a parcel of land where a network will be located. For this reason, it is efficient for a government to decide the location of a grid of public space before private-sector development takes place, especially in advance of the extensive capital investments that characterize urban development.

One successful example of this kind of sequencing is the Commissioner's Plan of 1811 for New York City. It laid out a grid of public space for infrastructure on the undeveloped agricultural land of Manhattan above what is now known as Houston Street. This grid extended all the way up to 155th Street. Without even exercising the right of eminent domain, this plan notified landowners that when the streets and avenues were eventually developed, the landowners would not be compensated for the structures built after the plan was implemented on land where a future street or avenue would be located.

One of the reasons why the Commissioner's Plan was so successful is that it specified a generous allocation of public space for infrastructure, more than 30% of the surface area of the land (not including land devoted to parks and open space). In addition, the plan allowed for a temporal separation between the specification of the land that would be used for infrastructure and the actual expenditures that would eventually be required to build the infrastructure. In fact, it took nearly 100 years for sidewalks and roads to be built on all of the grid's streets and avenues.

Public land is essential to the grid of network infrastructure needed to support urban life. Organizations such as the Urbanization Project at NYU Stern are helping fast-growing cities in the developing world follow a version of the planning approach that worked so well in New York City. To make the task more manageable, the process lays out in advance only an arterial grid with a separation between trunk roads of about 1 kilometer. These arteries should allow roads between them wide enough so that, in coming decades, they can support both passenger buses and other vehicles as well as the subsurface locations for water and sewer mains.

Different states vary substantially in their capacity to assemble land for new network infrastructure projects. Compare, for example, two former British colonies: Singapore, which has an unusually aggressive eminent domain law, and India, where historically it has been difficult for the government to use its legal right to eminent domain. Singapore today has perhaps the world's finest infrastructure, whereas India's infrastructure remains chronically underdeveloped relative to the country's needs.

This variation is not highly correlated with the level of development that a country can attain. The major infrastructure projects completed on time and on budget in China or France would be almost unthinkable in the US today, where even the redevelopment of obsolete and even dangerous infrastructure can involve years of debate, approvals, impact statements, legal challenges and appeals, and other blockages. If infrastructure is important, part of the US growth slowdown during the last decade (the slowest economic recovery since 1949) could be attributed to special interests scrapping over slices of a stagnant pizza rather than pouring political and economic effort into baking a larger pie and sharing the gains. American infrastructure development today seems to be decentralized and localized — coupled to federal support and commercial projects in the private sector — with the 1956 Eisenhower-era Interstate Highway System the sole postwar "grand design" initiative.

4.2 Ownership

A central legal issue in infrastructure development concerns the choice of ownership. Classically, infrastructure projects have been owned and financed by governments, at either the national or municipal level. In the past 30 years, however, privatization and investor ownership have emerged as a strong worldwide trend in projects as diverse as water systems, toll roads, tunnels, and power generation. Some projects use a mix of public and private partnerships (PPPs), indirect subsidies such as land grants, or the award of long-term franchise rights to a private operating company.

Private infrastructure ownership creates moral hazard problems related to long-term maintenance and risk taking. Private owners also benefit from a "holdup" problem, because they know that governments will provide bailouts for troubled entities as a result of their enormous positive externalities.

At the same time, private equity capital tends to view infrastructure projects as poor collateral, because such projects usually cannot be relocated or repurposed. Private owners put little value on residual claims. Some of the most spectacular financial infrastructure failures in advanced economies, such as Enron in the US or the Eurotunnel in Britain and France, can be attributed to high-risk, short-term infrastructure management strategies by private operators.

Although ownership choice can be viewed as a purely economic problem, in practice it is often clouded by political considerations. Two of the most obvious are nationalism and homeland security. Many countries require local ownership of infrastructure as a platform for showcasing the society's achievements whilst also providing employment opportunities for construction trades, engineers, professional managers and the politically connected.

Moreover, assets such as ports and electrical grids are deemed "strategic" and ruled off-limits to foreign ownership. For example, the US refused to allow Dubai's sovereign wealth fund to invest in American East Coast ports in 2006, and Greece strongly resisted control of its Piraeus cargo facilities by the Chinese state-own shipping giant COSCO until there was no longer a realistic alternative. Even when international or domestic private ownership is permitted, expropriation risk of infrastructure remains a clear issue. There is a long history of nationalizations and expropriations in sectors such as energy and transportation around the world.

The communications infrastructure industry has become an interesting focus of increased public oversight in the emerging era of "big data". Telephonic and computer networks' potential for use in government surveillance has stimulated debates about tradeoffs between privacy and law enforcement, especially in the advanced Western democracies.

In an age of terrorism, the potential value of surveillance and deterrence is unknowable, and people differ widely in the value they place on privacy versus security. So classic cost-benefit analysis is hard to apply. Both government and private communications infrastructure operators, who may have little business interest in these issues, find that complying with politically driven information-access regulation can become costly and raises difficult reputational questions, especially when human lives are at stake.

4.3 Regulation of Pricing

Many infrastructure projects become monopolists in a market for public necessities, and as a result they tend to face rate-of-return regulation. The pitfalls of the regulatory process almost certainly deter private investors from committing capital to long-term infrastructure projects. Modern pricing and monitoring systems, such as variable intraday pricing for electrical use or congestion-based highway tolls, offer great promise in this area, but politicians and the public often resist them. People do not like to pay market prices for infrastructure services, preferring to pass the true cost to others through the fiscal system. Some countries have overcome this blockage much better than others.

Regulators' goals can be complex and change often, as tradeoffs occur between delivering acceptable risk-adjusted rates of return to investors and affordable services to the public. Often this process is compromised by political gatekeepers who see an opportunity for graft, as well as labor unions that have the power to alter consumer pricing by threatening to shut down infrastructure that provides key public goods.

Infrastructure operators' ability to enforce contracts in order to collect revenue from their customers is often dubious. For example, theft of electrical power is an endemic problem for utilities worldwide, because of the ease with which customers can splice into a system as well as the difficulty for operators of identifying the perpetrators and beneficiaries. In impoverished cities and states, governments are loath to allow utilities to disconnect water or electricity for citizens who cannot pay their bills — in the US this was a major issue in the municipal bankruptcy of Detroit, to cite one well-known example.

4.4 Labor Relations

Organized labor plays a strong role in operating and maintaining infrastructure, especially in the transportation sector. Unions have been very successful in industries such as air travel and public transit because of relatively inelastic public demand for these services, as well as the fixed nature of many of the facilities (making union organization easier) and regulatory barriers to entry. The public necessity of these services has often created public political pressure to accede to union demands.

Inefficient operating practices and inflated wage structures have often resulted from union power, undermining transit systems' ability to maintain their capital stock and deliver services. Infrastructure operators may enjoy special legal protections against labor issues, such as bans on the right to strike or the ability to invoke government mediation. Sometimes even these protections are violated. For example, labor disruptions in public transport occur routinely in some European countries including strikes by unions that represent essential professions like air traffic controllers. The resulting revenue shortfalls and operating cost increases cast a shadow over competitive financing in debt and equity capital markets.

Labor relations play much less of a role in other infrastructure sectors such as electrical power and water delivery. These industries are much more capital intensive and in some sectors the role of labor has greatly diminished over time because of technological innovations, such as the containerization of shipping and the automation of highway toll collection.

4.5 Public Health and Safety

Because of their daily impact on the general public, infrastructure operators face some of the strongest public safety regulations of any industry. Active government oversight of the supply of infrastructure services is widely viewed as necessary to ensure the purity of drinking water, the security of transit passengers, and the safety of citizens who live near gas-fired or nuclear power plants. Other controversies, such as the purported dangers of living near high-tension power lines, pose theoretical threats that remain unproven but typically face a high degree of public risk aversion.

The implicit costs of public safety regulation have always affected the calculus of infrastructure projects. In recent years, the increased threat of terrorism has adversely changed the economics of transportation worldwide. Sectors such as water and electric power appear to have suffered less from regulatory drag, although in principle these arenas may be even more inviting for politically-driven disruption.

4.6 Environmental Regulation

Environmental impacts have long affected the economics of infrastructure projects — and hence their financing. Negative environmental externalities of such projects clearly need to be internalized, and these costs will be passed along to end-users and providers of capital. There is no free lunch. Under the well accepted "polluter pays principle", the resulting price and cost changes associated with environmental policy can lead to structural changes in consumption and resource allocation. How to best implement this principle is arguable, and the options range from physical pollution constraints to markets for environmental permits. But the so-called "general-equilibrium effects" on the economy — working with, not against, market forces — offer the best prospects for achieving optimal solutions.

Problems occur when environmental policies result in changing goalposts, generating additional risks for those providing capital to infrastructure projects and in some cases causing significant delays and cost overruns. Environmental impact assessments, in turn, can be heavily politicized and captured by "not in my backyard" advocates, sometimes blocking infrastructure projects altogether. Such assessments can also differ dramatically among countries, so that major infrastructure projects developed in, for example, France or China might be impossible in the US.

Increasing environmental regulation to address climate change likewise seems poised to become a critical legal problem for both new and existing infrastructure projects. Some facilities, such as coal-fired power plants, may be forced into obsolescence despite their economic viability. Other types of projects, such as those in mass transit or "clean" energy, may benefit from legal and political subsidies that increase their attractiveness to investors and local governments. International treaties and carbon trading schemes may upend the legal and financial basis of many infrastructure activities in coming years.

Developing environmental regulation of infrastructure seems as uncertain as it is important. Regulatory evolution may profoundly affect diverse entities such as water utilities in the southwestern United States and coal-fired power plants in China, whilst also influencing national decisions about the optimal amount of highway construction or commitments to nuclear power. The policy tradeoffs are extremely difficult — likely global warming from CO_2 emissions versus extremely low-probability accidents in zero-emissions nuclear facilities.

Taken together, the benchmarks for constructing and operating infrastructure will likely continue to expand the emphasis on environmental impact alongside customer service, public safety, and returns to investors. Assessing the associated benefits, costs, and risks will continue to increase the complexity of access to investable capital.

5. Beyond Economics: Governance and Infrastructure Development

In charting a course for financing infrastructure programs globally, many will argue for a focus on stable, democratic states where commercial financing is available, because the results will be more predictable and outcomes more favorable. But as governments address infrastructure development challenges, this perspective turns out to be too narrow. It fails to consider broader national policy interests as well as problems of limited governmental capacity to support development of needed infrastructure.

In the US, for example, the federal government recognizes the strategic importance of supporting key regional allies in the developing world, where infrastructure is essential to economic growth. So policymakers need to integrate efforts to finance infrastructure projects into this broader policy framework. Plans to increase infrastructure financing must include a mix of target countries, both strategically important developed states as well key strategic countries in less developed regions.

Substantial investments in infrastructure are essential to economic development. As countries industrialize, the need for infrastructure grows exponentially to meet the demands of increased commercial activity and growing populations.[1] Infrastructure can generate

---

1   See Kahale (2011).

predictable, long-term revenues that the host government can use to bolster education, health care, and other basic human rights.

Models for infrastructure financing differ dramatically, however, in countries with relatively weak governmental structures and safeguards. These countries struggle with poor governance, which results in a lack of public accountability and transparency as well as the absence of clear laws, independent courts, and well-functioning administrative and regulatory agencies. Such governments commonly impose crippling restrictions on civil society organizations and impede freedom of the press. These governance gaps result from years of control by arbitrary leaders who cannot or will not build a sustainable political and economic climate.

Infrastructure investments can support sustainability in less developed countries by strategically and honestly addressing these critical governance gaps. The inconvenient truth is that governance gaps form the greatest impediment to developing and financing basic physical infrastructure projects in these countries (roads, ports, and electrical power supplies). They create instability and risk that must be built into the cost of infrastructure finance, and these factors sometimes can deter investors entirely or cut the likelihood of completion on existing projects. Even when a government guarantees to cover various project risks, the guarantees are only as good as the guarantor.

The link between weak governance and lack of economic progress is clear. Each year, Transparency International surveys more than 175 countries and ranks them in its Corruption Perceptions Index. A poor score reflects widespread bribery, a lack of prosecution or punishment for official corruption, and public institutions that fail to respond to citizens' needs. Unsurprisingly, failing states such as North Korea and Somalia rank at the bottom of this index, but so do Burma (Myanmar), Haiti, Iraq, and Afghanistan — all places where developed-country policymakers are working to support economic growth and promote greater stability and progress by developing infrastructure.

A disproportionately large number of the most corrupt states are in Africa, including key regional players such as Nigeria which ranked 136 of the 167 countries in the 2015 Corruption Perceptions Index. The World Bank's repeated efforts to encourage governance reforms in countries where it engages in projects show how important and difficult governance reforms are to achieve. Despite attempts to cut the "leakage" of its financings into bribery, corruption, and offshore accounts, projects are still left to support debt service that produced no value

Another key indicator of sustainability is the rule of law. In recent years, the American Bar Association helped to launch the World Justice Project, which now publishes an annual Rule of Law Index. Still in its early iterations and with insufficient data to analyze many countries, the 2015 index covers 102 nations. It analyzes factors such as the presence of independent courts and administrative agencies, a clear and transparent lawmaking process, and access to legal remedies within each society.

Unsurprisingly, countries such as Venezuela and Iran rate very low, but so do several key US and European allies such as Nigeria (96), Kenya (84), and Egypt (86). A significant number of African states that fared poorly in Transparency International's corruption index do not publish enough data for inclusion in the Rule of Law Index, but it is safe to assume they also would score very poorly.

The effect of poor governance on economic development is striking. In 2014, the World Bank ranked 185 countries according to various development indicators, including per capita income. At the bottom were countries such as the Central African Republic and the Democratic Republic of the Congo. The 20 poorest countries on the World Bank's list are all in sub-Saharan Africa. Even key regional players with significant natural and human resources, such as Kenya (150) and Nigeria (123),were far down on the list.[2]

These rankings correspond with the aforementioned indexes rating elements of political sustainability such as corruption and the rule of law. They also underscore the enormity of the challenge in building successful sustainable economic models — including financing models for infrastructure development — absent fundamental political reforms.

Mindful of the risks in undertaking infrastructure project financing in such difficult places, the investment community has begun initiatives to develop and track social and environmental standards.

One prominent private-sector example is the Equator Principles (EPs), now in its third iteration. The EPs state that a financial institution

---

2   World Economic Outlook Database, April 2015, International Monetary Fund at https://www.imf.org/external/pubs/ft/weo/2015/01/weodata/index.aspx

engaged in project finance cannot provide loans or advisory services unless the sponsors can prove that they will meet minimum standards for determining, assessing, and managing environmental and social risks associated with the project.[3] Any risky projects must first complete an Environmental and Social Management Plan that includes mitigation, plans of action, monitoring, and management of any potential issues, as well as establishing grievance mechanisms if needed.[4] In addition, an independent expert must conduct an environmental and social impact review.[5] TAs of 2016, 78 financial institutions from 35 countries have adopted the EPs, representing 80% of total involvement in global project finance.[6]

Although the EPs are the best-known, other standards are also common in project financing. The EPs are based on International Finance Corporation (IFC) performance standards, which are also applied when IFC financing is secured for a project. Certain country-based initiatives may also apply. The Japan Bank for International Cooperation (JBIC), the Export-Import Bank of the US (Eximbank), and other export credit agencies have implemented their own guidelines.[7]

A criticism of these standards is that they lack independent oversight and risk becoming a routine reporting exercise without much substance. Some non-governmental organizations are critical of the EPs' oversight and implementation. The question of how to handle non-compliance with the EPs by participating financial institutions remains unresolved. Many of these standards are far more robust with respect to environmental guidelines than they are to human rights.

On a specific policy level, President Obama made infrastructure development in Africa a high priority for his administration. In a 2013 speech in Cape Town, he announced "Power Africa", a program that in his words would provide "a light where currently there is darkness, the energy need to lift people out of poverty". Power Africa was the Obama administration's signature infrastructure initiative in Africa, a

---

3   Equator Principles, http://www.equator-principles.com
4   *Ibid.*
5   *Ibid.*
6   https://www.cigionline.org/sites/default/files/no24_0.pdf
7   See, e.g., https://www.jbic.go.jp/en/efforts/environment, http://www.exim.gov/policies/ex-im-bank-and-the-environment/environmental-and-social-due-diligence-procedures-and-guidelines

$7 billion commitment coordinated by the Agency for International Development.[8]

The program's launch was hampered by difficulties in consummating power generation deals among African governments and private companies. Power Africa was intended to promote private investment rather than to provide direct government financial assistance. The US Eximbank was supposed to provide $5 billion in financing in the form of loans, loan guarantees, and insurance to help pay for American exports incorporated into the projects. Congressional debate in 2016 on whether to renew Eximbank's charter stalled US government funding for Power Africa.[9]

The problem in getting Power Africa off the ground, however, started at the local level. Consider the case of Nigeria, the continent's most populous country with more than 170 million people. Nigeria's vast oil reserves yield about 80% of government revenues. The combination of falling oil prices along with longstanding corruption and efficiency problems, however, severely hampered development. On a visit to Washington, the Nigerian head of state sought US assistance in helping recover stolen funds, and in an op-ed piece in the *Washington Post*, he said, "The fact that I now seek Obama's assistance in locating and returning $150 billion in funds stolen in the past decade and held in foreign bank accounts on behalf of former corrupt officials is testament to how badly Nigeria has been run".

In a July 2015 visit to Kenya and Ethiopia, President Obama admitted that Power Africa had fallen far short of its objectives. He laid much of the blame on debilitating governance failures in the countries concerned.

More recently, in a different part of the world, the Investment Fund of Malaysia (1MDB) was created as a sovereign wealth fund in 2009, not long after Najib Razak became Malaysia's prime minister. The fund aimed to promote economic development and foreign direct investment, as well as transform Kuala Lumpur into a global financial hub. Unlike other sovereign wealth funds, 1MDB was based not on government financial surpluses but rather on raising debt in global financial markets to acquire infrastructure assets.

---

8   Nixon, Ron. "Obama's 'Power Africa' Project Is Off to a Sputtering Start". *New York Times*, 21 July, 2015.

9   *Ibid.*

Bond issues undertaken by 1MDB — and led by Goldman Sachs against unusually high fees — rose to a peak of $11 billion by March 2014. Some of the proceeds were used to buy infrastructure assets such as power plants. Other funds flowed into joint ventures with international partners, such as Abu Dhabi and Saudi Arabia. Allegedly a significant share of the funds raised were diverted to various insiders — with several hundred million dollars going to Malaysian prime minister Najib's personal offshore bank accounts via various channels, including a small Swiss private bank. Mr. Najib denied wrongdoing, stating that some of the money was a personal gift from an unnamed Saudi donor, and that in any event most of the funds had been returned.

The case was dropped in Malaysia but remained under investigation in Switzerland and the US, where in July 2016 the Department of Justice issued a civil complaint alleging that $3.5 billion was siphoned from 1MDB for the personal benefit of various officials. For its part Goldman Sachs was alleged to have violated the 1970 US Bank Secrecy Act, which required financial intermediaries to do proper due diligence on clients and prevent money laundering.[10]

Whatever the 1MDB outcome, the lack of transparency and the level of corruption involved, the incremental risk faced *ex post* by debtholders, and the exposure of the Malaysian public to debt service that may not come close to being generated by the use of its capital, all highlight the reach of governance issues. Big-ticket infrastructure can be a scammers' honeypot, undermining the financial economics of otherwise viable projects, creating negative value for those required to meet future debt service obligations, and elevating the risks to which investors are exposed.

In the face of such challenges, some will argue that the US and other developed country governments' efforts to finance infrastructure projects should focus closer to home and on more stable democratic states where commercial financing is more available, transparency and legal protections are better and where results will likely be superior and more predictable. The opposing view argues that government-supported infrastructure projects should include a mix of target countries and that

---

10   Paddock (2016).

overcoming governance obstacles may lead to more general reforms and hence to benefits beyond the project economics themselves.

It may therefore be appropriate to support a mixed portfolio of infrastructure initiatives in target countries that starts with developed economies and extends to others undergoing political and social transitions. For the US, such a strategy could apply to countries such as Indonesia and Colombia, where a concerted effort to identify funding for infrastructure projects could support both economic and political development.

The global commitments to a low-carbon economy and the UN SDGs also help prioritize and build political support for financing infrastructure in specific countries. When economic support for infrastructure is framed in a larger context it can encourage continued political reform and democratization.

A second category of countries consists of key regional leaders, such as Kenya and Nigeria in Africa, although often these countries pose greater investment risks than more developed nations. In a country such as Nigeria, where weak government and widespread corruption have impeded economic progress for decades, the merging of political reform and economic support agendas is practical could prove to be wise.

A third and still more challenging category consists of countries with extremely weak governance that are at critical junctures of their transitions (e.g., Myanmar). Often the window to effectuate change in such nations is very narrow, and active outside engagement is needed to prevent backsliding. In such countries, government efforts to support infrastructure financing must be accompanied by diplomatic strategies that underscore the critical need for fundamental political reforms. By clearly articulating this strategy and acknowledging the inevitable risks, governments such as the US, can fulfill salutatory commitments to improve infrastructure in less developed countries whilst working to promote democratic governance models rooted in human rights, transparency, and the rule of law.

To appreciate the importance of the interaction between politics and economics in determining infrastructure outcomes, consider the case of electric power generation, the infrastructure subsector that arguably caused the most recent FDI bubble to turn out badly.

After a wave of privatization and (partial) deregulation around the world, more than $400 billion in FDI in power generation took place between 1992 and 2002 and allegedly led to more than $100 billion in value destruction.

From the US alone, 24 established utilities invested abroad during this period and, apart from two that exited at the crest of the investment wave, the remainder suffered an estimated –11% internal rate of return in the aggregate. Even worse, analysis of individual foreign investment projects undertaken by US utilities indicates that "high-status" firms (i.e., those with current or former directors or top managers of Fortune 500 firms on their boards) were particularly prone to large-scale FDI, and that neither equity analysts nor stock markets seemed to have much foresight about the viability of these projects.[11]

None of this should be particularly surprising. According to the international business historian Mira Wilkins, the electric power sector was one of the first to be subject to counterstrikes by national governments via nationalization of FDI in early 20th century Venezuela and in Russia after the Bolshevik Revolution.[12] Power generation is a prime example of a sector prone to governmental intervention and associated problems because of the business's relatively large size, large sunk costs, environmental externalities, public perceptions of entitlement and systemic effects on the rest of the economy. Even without nationalization or expropriation, losses can be visited on foreign infrastructure investors through price controls and other regulatory measures.

Of course, many of the same points about business characteristics apply to other infrastructure verticals. For these reasons, infrastructure finance involves — or should involve — astute consideration of political economy alongside project economics.

---

11   Hill and Thomas (2005).
12   Hausman, Hertner, and Wilkins (2008).

6. The Global Infrastructure Development Sector

Studies of global infrastructure development often omit a perspective on the infrastructure development industry itself. Infrastructure development is the industry that turns infrastructure ideas into physical reality — contractors, engineering firms, hardware suppliers, and so on. Consequently, market penetration, cost functions, scale and scope economies, and other competitive variables that characterize infrastructure development have a direct effect on its economics. Vibrant competition among suppliers in executing infrastructure projects to the highest possible standards at the lowest possible cost is in the interests of the various project stakeholders — lenders, investors, and end users.

Available data covering the global cluster of the top 250 infrastructure contractors worldwide suggests that the sector is much more interregional than is typical for most global industries. US-based contractors rank 17th in the cohort of these 250 firms. Geopolitics, although relatively insignificant for most industries, thus becomes highly relevant for infrastructure project execution.

A concrete example involves China, which in recent years seems to have gained the most in its share of the global infrastructure development market, and the US, which appears to have lost more share than any other single country during the same period. The value proposition of successful Chinese competitors in this space relative to their US rivals centers mainly on lower prices. There are several possible explanations for this dynamic.

Lower absolute costs of capital equipment. As in other manufacturing categories, China holds significant absolute cost advantages in terms of capital equipment thanks to well-developed and improving supply chains, as well as low labor and capital costs. Cost levels are thought to be at least 10% to 20% lower for basic categories of capital goods compared with Western suppliers.

Lower absolute costs of labor. Absolute competitive advantages embedded in equipment costs are augmented by lower labor costs for on-site construction services. The usual Chinese practice in Africa, for instance, is to bring in Chinese workers for construction, which generates significant savings relative to the Western practice of relying mostly on local labor. The Chinese approach sometimes incurs local political resentment, but it helps assure that that an entire project operates from the same well-rehearsed playbook.

Lower costs of capital. Especially for Chinese state-owned enterprises (SOEs), capital costs are often very low given higher-level objectives related preserving (or ideally, augmenting) employment and political gains deemed to be in China's national interest. In addition to reducing the costs embedded in local capital equipment, lower capital costs decrease the markup that contractors must charge to break even economically on the amount of capital they deploy.

Economies of scale. China has been the largest, most rapidly growing national construction services market in the world, whereas the US and Europe both exhibit declining shares. Static scale economies, as well as the opportunities that growth offers, enable Chinese competitors to deploy the latest technology in their own operations (vintage effects), which should complement the absolute advantages identified above. And the predicted long-term eastward shift of the world's center of economic gravity, from the North Atlantic toward Asia-Pacific, can only amplify the effects of realizable economies of scale.

Coordination gains. In the presence of monopoly power — and by extension market power — coordination may enhance competitiveness relative to a benchmark in which, say, potential equipment suppliers and potential financiers set their terms independently of each other. The Chinese model involves more coordination of this sort than the US model (where, for example, the Export-Import Bank has come under threat), and Chinese international economic engagement is often seen as an extension of international political engagement.

Subsidization. Chinese practice often seems to go well beyond exploiting complementarities to building a subsidy component into infrastructural deals for a range of reasons. Absorbing excess foreign exchange reserves exposed (until recently) the nation's apparent desire to move beyond being a "lonely power" without close allies to prioritize capital goods as the next stage in its ascent of the technology ladder. Public commitments to foreign infrastructure are also contained for example, in the announcement of the New Silk Road and the formation of the Asian Infrastructure Investment Bank

Articulating all of these potential sources of lower infrastructure execution costs should help explain why US and European competitor claims of Chinese underpricing by 50% or more are not outlandish. China's competitors have their own value propositions, however, which revolve around some distinct sources of differentiation. Here are some concrete examples:

Quality. Quality advantages can help offset US, Japanese, and European competitors' price disadvantages against Chinese rivals. Compare Caterpillar and Komatsu competing with Chinese construction equipment leader Sany. In advanced economies, contractors buy heavy equipment based on quality and expect it to last for decades. In China, poorly capitalized local enterprises, often linked to corrupt officials, buy the cheapest machines possible and rent them out to local contractors on a job-by-job basis. So Sany builds a cheaper, less durable design and sells (with attractive financing) in this price-sensitive segment. Caterpillar and Komatsu cater more to quality-sensitive purchasers [Hout and Michael, 2014]. The Chinese saying that equipment needs only to be "good enough" reflects many of these attributes.

Learning advantages. Western competitors may, along some dimensions, hold advantages over Chinese rivals that the latter must surmount over time rather than in the short term. For instance, Chinese manufacturers have mastered relatively simple manufacturing, involving fewer than a thousand parts per product, but they still lag Western competitors in systems integration capabilities and software development, as well as in manufacturing systems with far more parts (e.g., aircraft engines, high-speed rail networks, and nuclear power reactors).[1]

More sophisticated management approaches may also play a role in the Chinese learning advantage. For instance, US-based Cummins develops and manufactures diesel engine families with varying prices and features around the world. Cummins leads within China in the higher-performance segment and can, because of its distributed production and R&D capabilities, ship more engines into China than it ships out (both highly advanced and lower-priced varieties). Such global operating architectures and sourcing flexibility require internationally experienced middle managers, subtle cross-border coordination mechanisms, and technical depth in many locations that can be built only with time.

Technological upgrading. The effect of lags can be extended by continuing to upgrade and raise the bar for less (vertically) differentiated competitors. This idea is consistent with traditional literature on the multinational enterprise, and John Sutton recently explored it in the context of global escalation games.[2] A study of competition between Western and Chinese firms through this lens looks broadly within China, at 44 industries in which foreign competition is allowed, and finds that non-Chinese firms (e.g., Corning, GE, Intel, Pfizer, and Merck) lead in 10 of the 13 industries in which R&D exceeds 6% of sales.[3] The Chinese government has taken many measures to force more technology transfer to local firms (Hout and Ghemawat, 2010). A study of competition between Western and Chinese firms through this lens looks broadly within China, at 44 industries in which foreign competition is allowed, and finds that non-Chinese firms (e.g., Corning, GE, Intel, Pfizer, and Merck) lead in 10 of the 13 industries in which R&D exceeds 6% of sales.[4]

Compliance expertise. Another potential advantage has to do with Western competitors' generally superior ability to comply with the procurement, environmental, and other standards. Chinese competitors

1   Nomura Securities (2014).
2   Caves (1971); Sutton (2012).
3   Ghemawat and Hout (forthcoming).
4   Hout and Ghemawat (2010); Ghemaway and Hout (2016).

generally admit to being well behind in this regard. Nonetheless, the Chinese looseness in this arena, such as the lack of an equivalent to the US Foreign Corrupt Practices Act, may actually help Chinese companies in some ways. Strict anticorruption measures may well be socially optimal, although not necessarily from the (private) perspective of a competitor. For this situation to change in countries that rank worst on indexes related to corruption or lack of transparency will require a fundamental transformation at the local level, although global anti-corruption initiatives can play an important supporting role.

This discussion highlights the roles of governmental policies and managerial decision-making in determining how competitive positions in infrastructure execution may evolve over time. It implies, for Western companies and governments, a strategy based on selectivity rather than across-the-board competition, and a shift from the pursuit of market share to economic value maximization.

7. Infrastructure Finance

So far, this study has considered generic infrastructure development issues — ranging from greenfield projects in developing countries to the redevelopment and maintenance of aging and obsolete infrastructure in advanced countries — that have significantly hindered economic and social progress. Infrastructure also figures heavily in urbanization, a global phenomenon, and the development of grid-based "smart cities" intended to facilitate the accompanying shifts in both population and economic activity locations. As discussed, infrastructure development issues differ equally dramatically in areas such as eminent domain, reliance on market versus command mechanisms, bribery and corruption, and the state of civil society.

We considered the nature of infrastructure projects; some of the uniqueness and challenges in the underlying dynamics, including scale and the role of externalities; and the legal dimensions and globalization of infrastructure activities including sustainability and governance issues. We now turn specifically to project and infrastructure finance — how to link sources and uses of investable funds worldwide to most efficiently finance infrastructure development and maintenance.

Next, we shall examine two separate issues. First, how can global banking and capital markets provide a cost-effective financial "air supply" for financially viable infrastructure initiatives whilst denying capital to projects that are not viable? Second, how can the financial instruments created by infrastructure finance be placed with institutional investors that are trying to optimize portfolios and meet fiduciary obligations to their own clients?

To address these questions, we consider the mechanics of project finance and the role of financial instruments and markets, and we explore their debt-like and equity-like characteristics as an asset class. We present some encouraging empirical results on infrastructure financing returns and risks from the perspective of global investors. We also conclude, however, that the techniques and markets needed to transform financing for large-scale infrastructure initiatives into financial instruments suffer from "clogs" that impede progress. New approaches are needed to combine the return, liquidity, and risk attributes that investors and fiduciaries seek in a way that allows infrastructure finance via the global capital markets to reach its full potential.

We begin by building on the extensive infrastructure literature that already exists.[1]

Infrastructure finance is one of the most complex and challenging dimensions of the global financial architecture. Equity and debt, bank lending and bond markets, foreign exchange and derivatives must all come together in an understandable way in order to unlock the underlying potential of infrastructure projects — and to deny funding for those projects incapable of demonstrating viability. Project returns to investors must account for an array of interrelated risks ranging from completion risk and market risk to sovereign risk and *force majeure* risk. In addition, the instruments emanating from project financing must fit the portfolio-efficiency objectives of major capital pools worldwide, including bank lending portfolios and the asset profiles of pension funds and other institutional investors.

We aim to combine the foregoing substantive discussion of the role of infrastructure development and its financing at one end of a spectrum with the requisites of investor portfolio optimization at the other. Shortcomings in the global financial architecture that forms key linkages across this spectrum are associated with both explicit costs and opportunity costs that affect economic efficiency as well as growth. Here we explore these shortcomings and attempt to address them through a set of policy-related conclusions. We also provide anecdotal evidence,

---

1   See, for example, World Economic Forum (2014).

however, that suggests the financing available today may outstrip the supply of financeable infrastructure projects.[2]

Project and infrastructure finance has existed for hundreds of years, mainly in the form of production payment loans and, more broadly, limited-recourse lending. All of the 17th century European trading companies, such as the Dutch East India Company, financed their maritime expeditions by borrowing to underwrite the cost of a specific voyage and then repaying investors if, and only if, the fleet returned and selling the cargo proved profitable.

Emergence of project financing approaches has differed widely around the world. In the US, for instance, project finance schemes first began to appear for the construction of railroads and other transportation infrastructure in the late 19th century, as well as in the financing of high-risk exploration wells by independent oil companies during the 1920s and 1930s. In the second half of the 20th century, this financing technique evolved and became more widely used in the private sector for many high-risk, capital-intensive projects such as independent power plants, commercial real estate complexes, large oil and gas development fields, and mining.

Over time, governments also adopted project finance techniques to fund public infrastructure, including toll roads, bridges, tunnels, stadiums, and airports. Many such projects were financed with general obligation (GO) bonds or their equivalent, backed by the full faith and credit of the government sponsor. Increasingly, however, such on-balance-sheet obligations have been replaced by industrial development bonds (IDBs) and industrial revenue bonds (IRBs), specifically backed by cash flows from the underlying project.

More recently, government budgetary pressures have given rise to various innovative financing structures allowing for a greater private-sector role in constructing and operating large-scale public service projects. Such public-private partnerships (PPPs), pioneered by European governments, took the form of build-operate-transfer (BOT),

---

2   For example, an interesting new financing approach and asset class seems to be emerging in the form of green bonds and other financing mechanisms aimed at tackling green infrastructure, such as watershed protection and storm-water capture, renewable energy microgrids and storage, and sustainable transportation grids in cities. Some of this need will require aggregating smaller units (such as residences) and distributing finance through historically less creditworthy entities.

build-own-operate (BOO), and design-build-finance-operate (DBFO) arrangements.

In the last 20 years, project and infrastructure finance accelerated and spread from the industrialized world to emerging markets. Both the globalization of the world's financial markets and the adoption of growth-oriented, market-based economic policies in many developing countries fed this infrastructure finance boom. Foreign-direct and portfolio investors sought out higher-return projects and cross-border exposure diversification in emerging markets, particularly in the energy, power, and telecommunications sectors.

Meanwhile, deregulation and stepped-up privatizations in host countries broadened the opportunity set for project and infrastructure finance. OECD estimates suggest that more than $400 billion of state-owned assets were privatized in developing countries between 1990 and the onset of the global financial crisis in 2007.

The infrastructure finance arena has faced some headwinds, such as the 1997–1998 Asian financial crisis, the 2001–2002 global recession, the Argentine sovereign debt default in December 2001, and a general rise in nationalism, punctuated by several high-profile Venezuelan and Russian energy project expropriations. Nonetheless, infrastructure project finance activity has remained robust for decades.

Project finance is narrowly defined as "the raising of funds on a limited-recourse or non-recourse basis to finance an economically-separable capital investment project, in which the providers of the funds look primarily to the cash flow from the project as the source of funds to service their loans and provide an acceptable return on equity invested in the project".[3]

Given the large capital requirements involved, financing such deals typically involves multiple funding sources, usually consisting mainly of debt. Most private-sector infrastructure projects are financed with an average 70/30 mix of debt and equity, compared with a typical 50/50 mix in the corporate arena.[4] The debt component of public-sector infrastructure projects is typically substantially higher than for private-sector infrastructure projects, although in some cases (e.g., the Eurotunnel), equity in the project's special-purpose vehicle (SPV) may

---

3   Finnerty (2013).
4   For more detail, see Tice and Walter (2013).

be sold directly to public investors with shares listed on stock exchanges. Figure 3 profiles the key contractual and financial components of infrastructure projects.

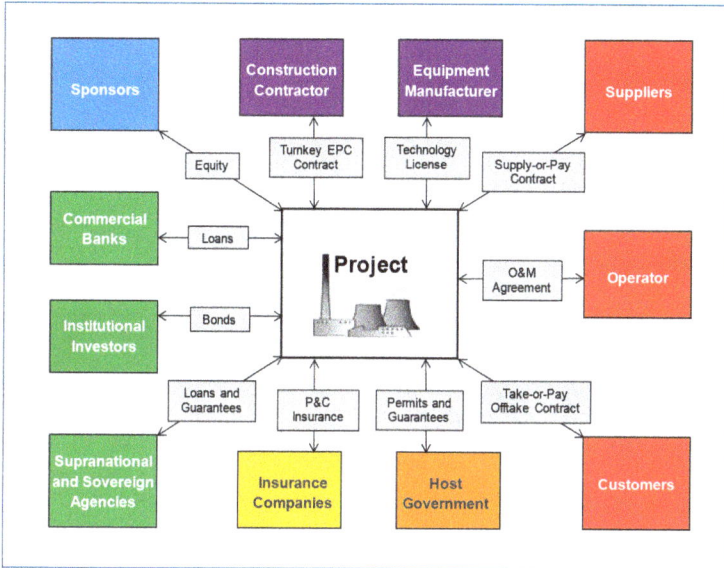

Figure 3. Prototype Project Finance Structure (Source: Tice and Walter [2014] based on Smith, Walter and De Long [2012])

Based on this definition, three important aspects of project and infrastructure finance distinguish it from other financing approaches:

1. The asset being financed is a long-lived capital asset.

2. The project's sponsors establish and become principal shareholders in an SPV, thereby de-consolidating the project from their respective public- or private-sector balance sheets.

3. As a standalone legal entity, the SPV's debt is structured without recourse to the sponsors, thus preserving their credit quality.

8. Structuring the Financial Mosaic

Depending on the SPV sponsors' risk tolerance, the equity component of total financing may take one of two forms. It can be straight equity, funded by balance sheet cash in the case of a corporate sponsor, or by budgetary resources in the case of a government sponsor. It can also consist of shareholder loans that represent a more senior claim in the capital structure relative to equity and will need to be repaid.

On the debt side, commercial bank loans have traditionally provided a key source of funding for most projects, supplemented by credit facilities from multilateral development banks (e.g., the World Bank and the Asian Development Bank) and sovereign lenders (e.g., Export Development Canada, Germany's Hermes, and Mexico's Nacional Financiera), as well as bonds placed with institutional investors (mainly insurance companies and pension funds) and lease financing arrangements.

The overall infrastructure finance debt mix tends to be diversified by lender, maturity, and currency. It is usually balanced between floating- and fixed-rate borrowings, with a heavy emphasis on the former to minimize interest rate risk during the often extended life of a project.

Typically, bank loans are used almost exclusively during a project's higher-risk construction phase. These loans can then be partially replaced with fixed-rate bonds once a project begins to generate cash. Syndicated bank loans can be tailored to a project's specific needs to provide for construction cost overruns, delays, and other contingencies. *In extremis*, they can be restructured without triggering an event of default. The key role of bank lending highlights the need for loan syndicates to involve experienced banks that understand project risks and demonstrate the necessary discipline under adverse conditions, led by a highly reputed agent bank.

Loans provided by commercial banks priced at a fixed margin above floating-rate US dollar LIBOR or Euribor benchmarks, plus loans from Aaa/AAA rated multilateral development banks and highly rated sovereign agencies, typically represent the cheapest source of funding for any project. The latter, however, are usually capped at a relatively small percentage of overall project debt.

Any government guarantees in such financings put the financial exposure of infrastructure projects back onto the government balance sheet, a scenario that non-recourse project finance is designed to avoid. Most project debt is rated investment grade (low BBB or higher) and ranks as "senior secured", although unsecured, subordinated, and mezzanine debt tranches are also possible.

Given the multiple debt counterparties involved in project and infrastructure financings, inter-creditor agreements, covenant packages, and debt service reserve accounts are all important negotiating points. Most such financings are document-intensive transactions that require significant time and effort to close. As a result, structuring, advisory, and commitment fees all tend to be higher and lending margins wider compared to straight public corporate debt issuances and certainly compared to sovereign debt finance.

From a public- or private-sector sponsor's perspective, the final mix of project and infrastructure finance is designed to maximize total outstanding debt whilst minimizing overall financing costs, thus preserving the level of returns to shareholders and minimizing the exposure of public finance.

9. Identification and Mitigation of Project-related Risks

Risk identification, calibration, and mitigation are central to project and infrastructure finance. As noted, for the government or corporate sponsor involved, the main objective is to move a project's construction, operating, and financial risks off the balance sheet whilst maintaining control and capturing the economic upside — financial and, in the case of government, economic and social. For the creditors involved, because there is often no financial recourse to the project's sponsors, the primary goal is to ensure a stable source of cash flow to service the outstanding debt whilst safeguarding their standing in the cash-flow "waterfall" and collateral rights within the project's overall capital structure.

Given the multiple parties and myriad risks involved, most project and infrastructure financings are highly structured transactions. The nature of the risks in a large-scale capital project changes as the project moves from its construction phase (typically 1 to 5 years) to its longer-term operating phase (generally 25 to 30 years or longer).[1]

During construction, the main risks are that the project might be completed behind schedule, incur cost overruns, or fail to achieve commercial acceptance for technical reasons.

Once a project begins operations, the key risk is that projected cash flows might fall short of expectations because of weak demand, price pressures, or higher-than-anticipated operating and maintenance capital costs.

---

1   For a detailed discussion, see Smith, Walter and De Long (2012).

In the long term, potential risks include production issues (i.e., unplanned outages) and *force majeure* such as earthquakes, hurricanes, or terrorist attacks. All projects are exposed to sovereign or political risk during their entire life cycle, regardless of the nature of government involvement in their financing.

As discussed earlier in this study, infrastructure projects are intended to be significant direct and derivative contributors to national or local economic performance and stable generators of cash flow in the long term. Therefore, from the perspective of debt or equity capital providers, infrastructure projects are potential stationary targets for the host government — not only at a national level but in many cases state and local. Such political risk — generally termed "sovereign risk" at the national level — can range from increased taxation and other fiscal or regulatory regime changes to pressure to renegotiate contract terms (particularly if a government agency is a project counterparty) to outright expropriation.

Political risk tends to increase once a project starts operations and begins to generate cash. This risk is of special concern for projects in lower-rated emerging market countries with shaky lender and investor protections unless it can be mitigated by alternative governing law or external guarantees.

Political risk in infrastructure financing can be addressed in a variety of ways, including purchase of political risk insurance covering the capital structure, as well as participation of influential banks from several different countries (particularly major trading partners or creditors of the host country), regional development banks, or the World Bank. Sometimes a country's continued need for balance of payments financing, including rollovers of maturing debt, may give lenders and investors sufficient implied leverage to constrain adverse political moves.

At the project level, sources of risk to lenders and investors in infrastructure financing sometimes relate only to completion of a project. Alternatively, these risk sources may be longer term and could affect the project's operation for many years.

Evaluating and reducing both completion and operating risk requires expertise and ingenuity. Financial management of these risks generally relies on various guarantees. These may be direct (full and unqualified commitment on the part of the guarantor); limited in terms of amount or duration; or contingent, involving relatively unlikely events that lenders want mitigated in order to secure their participation. Guarantees may be either implied as an obligation of the guarantor or indirect via performance of some related activities that will, in effect, make the lender whole in the event of problems.

Lenders and investors also face completion risks, which are the focus of the sponsor's own evaluation of the technical challenges involved in successfully bringing a project on-line. These risks are assessed in-house and by engineering consultants or other outside experts. The sponsors, operators' and EPC contractors' track records of successfully undertaking comparable projects elsewhere are important in such assessments.[2] Projects involving new technologies or particularly adverse conditions (e.g., climatic or topological) tend to multiply completion risks.

Lenders may require completion guarantees from project sponsors to unconditionally warrant that performance will be as specified (in terms of quantity, quality, timing, and minimum period of operation) and that the sponsors will cover any and all cost overruns. Sponsors may be asked in advance to agree to specific tests of physical and economic completion, with lender recourse lapsing only after these tests have been satisfactorily met. Cost-sharing arrangements may oblige sponsors to carry a specific pro rata share of all project outlays, including debt service payments.

Sponsors may also provide "comfort letters", sometimes called "letters of moral intent" or "keepwells". Without issuing a formal guarantee, these letters promise that the sponsor will supervise and maintain an active interest in the vehicle company throughout the project's pre-completion and operating phases. Such documents, however, even when tightly worded, cannot be viewed as guarantees.

Following project completion, market risk (notably the risk of revenue shortfalls) in infrastructure financings can be met by "take-or-pay" contracts, whereby the ultimate purchasers unconditionally commit themselves to make specific payments for a given period, whether or not they actually take delivery of the project's products or

---

2   EPC contractors refer to firms responsible for project engineering, procurement and construction.

services. One problem with take-or-pay contracts is that, in effect, the sponsor sacrifices a certain degree of control over the facility. Because the guarantor may be a third party, this approach can involve somewhat higher financing costs.

Infrastructure financing providers can sometimes also obtain "deficiency guarantees" covering an entire venture, either from the sponsors or from the government of the country where the project is located, or perhaps from the sponsors' home-country governments. Some guarantees cover losses of principal and interest suffered by lenders after any collateral has been liquidated in the event of default. In the case of a government's sovereign guarantee, country risk assessment will determine the guarantee's true value.

Collateral itself can take many forms, such as a lender's mortgage over the borrower's license or project facilities, assignment of interests in various agreements and contracts, assignment of insurance proceeds, assignment and liens on revenues generated or inventories and accounts receivable, contingent claims on financial accounts, or pledges of borrowers' equity shares.

In addition, sponsors may be committed to maintaining their financial interest in a venture at or above a specified level. Sellers of equipment to the project and/or their export credit agencies may also be willing to provide certain guarantees. The existence of a complex of guarantees provides support for infrastructure financing only to the extent that the guarantors are able and willing to meet their obligations. Each guarantor must therefore be subject to careful due diligence with respect to both "ability" and "willingness".

In essence, lenders and investors in project and infrastructure financings have to decide which of these risks are "bankable" and which must be covered by contractual arrangements with either project sponsors or third parties such as suppliers, customers, governments, or international organizations. In general, the rule is, "Manage the risks you know, and sell the rest".

To that end, contractual agreements are the main instrument for mitigating risk throughout the life of a project. During the construction phase, sponsor completion guarantees and fixed-price, turnkey EPC contracts (with contingency cushions) are often used to ensure projects are completed on time and on budget. During the operating phase, take-or-pay off-take and supply agreements related to infrastructure services are typically used to minimize project cash flow volatility and margin pressures, whereas insurance contracts are used to mitigate the risk of business interruption and total casualty loss.

To ameliorate sovereign risk, multilateral development banks and sovereign lenders are often deliberately included in the capital structure, along with political risk insurance policies and offshore cash lockboxes. The choice of governing law and arbitration forum for settling legal disputes is also a key risk mitigation technique.

In summary, a central function in infrastructure financing is to identify and quantify the various risks and then structure the deal to allocate those risks acceptably among the various participants. As financial institutions and investors enhance their understanding of the risks in particular types of projects, they may become increasingly prepared to accept a larger share of total project risks, which could mean less onerous covenants and guarantees for project sponsors. A reputable sponsor with a good record should be able to negotiate over a broad range of risks.

The fundamental challenge facing financial advisors on major projects is how to assemble a financing package that aligns all parties' interests, given the available financing sources, the risks, and the options for reducing and shifting those risks. In the end, the infrastructure project's underlying viability tends to be the determining factor.

10. Intermediating Infrastructure Finance: Market Contours

Historically, barriers to entry into the project and infrastructure finance market have been significant. Many deals in this arena are highly complex and require sophisticated legal, tax, accounting, financial, and engineering skills. Furthermore, the size of many infrastructure project financings requires both large equity checks on the part of sponsors and large balance sheets on the part of project lenders. Although most project debt has been rated investment grade, the credit analysis involved, with its heavy emphasis on contracts and covenants, requires a skill set more commonly found in the high-yield or private equity markets.

10.1 Changing Sponsors and Infrastructure Funds

In recent years, the ranks of traditional project sponsors (i.e., governments and corporations) have expanded to include dedicated infrastructure funds managed by private equity firms (e.g., Alinda Capital Partners, Brookfield Asset Management, and Global Infrastructure Partners) as well as commercial and investment banks (e.g., Citi Infrastructure Investors, GS Infrastructure Partners, and Morgan Stanley Infrastructure). Most of these funds target an internal rate of return of 8% to 15% or higher, and they charge both management fees (typically 1% to 2%) and performance fees (usually 10% to 20%).

Many of these private equity-style funds compete aggressively for project and infrastructure deals. For example, in January 2005, the Macquarie Infrastructure Group (MIG), an infrastructure fund managed by Australia's Macquarie Bank, was the high bidder on the 12.5-kilometer elevated Chicago Skyway Toll Bridge System, a concession that included responsibility for paying all operating and maintenance costs, as well as the right to receive all toll revenues, during a 99-year lease period. MIG's $1.8 billion all-cash bid, submitted through a joint venture with Spain's Cintra (a private developer of transport infrastructure), was roughly double the amount of the cover bid on the Chicago Skyway concession. The MIG fund was subsequently converted into a listed fund, Macquarie Atlas Roads Limited.

Listings by infrastructure fund managers have become common, particularly in the United Kingdom, Canada, and Australia. At present, there are roughly 50 listed infrastructure funds outstanding. Sovereign wealth funds, such as the China Investment Corporation, and government investment arms, such as Singapore's Temasek Holdings, likewise participate in project equity syndicates, either directly or indirectly through fund structures.

10.2 The Market for Project and Infrastructure Debt

From 2003 through 2015, the market for project finance debt (loans and bonds) roughly tripled in size, from $100–150 billion to approximately $350–400 billion. This growth came from a combination of aging infrastructure and public services in the developed world, strong economic performance and pressing development needs in the emerging markets, and fiscal constraints along with new government-sponsored initiatives in the area of renewable energy development.

The project loan market ($362 billion in 2015) was roughly 10 to 13 times larger than the project bond market ($27 billion in 2015), accounting for some 90% to 95% of total project finance debt issued from 2003 through 2015.

Most project loans and bonds were structured as amortizing secured debt and rated investment grade, either explicitly or implicitly, so as to minimize the required interest coupon. Sometimes credit enhancement products — such as insurance provided by companies such as Assured Guaranty, which guarantee the timely payment of interest and principal — were used to achieve targeted investment grade ratings.

Based on default and recovery rates tracked by Standard & Poor's from 1992 through 2014, investment-grade project finance debt experienced lower default rates and significantly higher recovery rates than equally rated senior secured and unsecured corporate debt.

The energy and electric power infrastructure sector accounted for nearly half of all project finance debt issuance (47%) from 2003 through 2015, with renewable projects (e.g., wind and solar power, ethanol, and biofuels) constituting an additional 13%. Renewable energy and power represented a growing percentage of the project finance debt market during the second half of this period, as an increasing number of governments implemented "green" policy mandates such as renewable power and renewable fuel standards.

Despite their high-profile government connections, renewable energy projects involve a unique set of risks for credit investors. For example, although solar and wind power have proven effective on a commercial scale, other green technologies remain commercially unproven. Another risk stems from the need for continuing political and fiscal support in the form of subsidies, tax credits, and/or "mandated" demand such as ethanol content in motor fuel to preserve projects' economics. The 2015 Paris Climate Accord, however, should increase incentives in the case of renewable power and distributed grids, reducing this risk.

Beyond traditional and alternative energy, the next-largest sector of the project and infrastructure finance debt market from 2003 through 2015 was shipping and transportation. This sector, including airports, roads, rail, and marine ports, accounted for roughly 21% of new debt issuance. The next 15 years are likely to see significant investment in water infrastructure worldwide, especially in arid regions, cities, and emerging economies.

Total project finance debt issuance was roughly evenly split between developed (52%) and emerging markets in Asia Pacific, Latin

America, Africa, and the Middle East (48%). Emerging market countries constituted a growing portion of overall volumes, as the Asia Pacific region (excluding Japan, Australia, and New Zealand) grew from 15%–20% during the 2003–2005 period to 30%–35% of all project finance debt during the 2010–2012 period, before declining to 20%–25% during the 2013–2015 period, mainly on the back of increased deal flow originating in China and India.[1]

10.3 The Key Role of Commercial Lending

Commercial banks constituted roughly 80% of the global project and infrastructure loan market, with supranationals (3%) and sovereign agencies (17%) accounting for the remainder.

The commercial bank loan segment of the infrastructure finance market has been dominated by large European and Japanese financial institutions. It has also been highly fragmented. The top 20 lead arrangers constituted only 40% to 45% of total loan issuance from 2003 through 2015, with most deals heavily syndicated.

From 2005 through 2007, bank lending margins narrowed to roughly LIBOR +50 bps to LIBOR +100 bps for many higher-quality projects. After the global financial crisis, they settled in the range of LIBOR +250 bps to LIBOR +350 bps.

Infrastructure and project finance commercial bank loans have traditionally been originated in "tranched" format[2] and then held on the lending bank's balance sheet until maturity. (Some up-front construction loans, however, are partially refinanced with fixed-rate bonds once a project is up and running.) The regulatory response to the crisis requiring commercial banks to hold higher capital levels, as well as more stringent liquidity and stable funding requirements, have further affected banks' critical role in providing debt financing for infrastructure projects.

---

1   McKinsey (2013) estimates that infrastructure spending in China and India (much of it government funded) averaged 8.5% and 4.7% of GDP, respectively, compared with approximately 2.6% of GDP in both the US and the European Community during 2010–2015.

2   This term refers to subordinated issues in an overall loan that vary as to currency, maturity, interest margin, and other characteristics.

10.4 The Infrastructure Bond Market

Most project and infrastructure bond financings have been sold as private placements to investment-grade investor accounts, mainly buy-and-hold insurance companies and pension funds that pursue asset-liability matching (i.e., longer-term assets to fund longer-term life insurance and pension claims). Some project finance bonds, however, are targeted toward high-yield investors such as hedge funds.

In investment-grade private placements of project and infrastructure debt, the intermediary bank serving as placement agent has typically charged a 0.875% to 1.000% fee. Distribution of the securities could follow either a traditional negotiated format[3] or a more public-style format designed to reach a larger investor base.[4]

Some of the large US insurance companies (e.g., American International Group, Allstate, John Hancock, MetLife, New York Life, Northwestern Mutual, and Prudential) have developed in-house private placement groups that focus specifically on project finance and infrastructure credits. These firms have typically taken the lead on, and driven demand for, investment-grade project and infrastructure bond deals.

Because institutional investors remain hesitant to take on construction risk, project finance and infrastructure bonds typically are not issued until a project moves out of its completion stage and starts generating cash flow (with the exception of brownfield projects that are already generating cash). Most private project finance bonds have been fixed rate (priced at a spread off the Treasury yield curve), longer dated (a 12- to 15-year average life), and relatively illiquid.

Although some bonds used in project and infrastructure finance have changed hands in the secondary market, trading activity has historically been infrequent and usually on an "order basis" by individual institutional investors. To compensate for the illiquidity and the extra analytical work involved in up-front due diligence, as well as the need for continuing credit monitoring, project finance bonds typically carry more yield than conventional publicly-issued investment-grade bonds.

---

3   In the US under Section 4(2) or SEC Regulation D securities law exemptions.
4   In the US under the terms of SEC Regulation 144A/Regulation S.

When pricing a new private project finance or infrastructure bond, the spread versus comparably rated corporate credits typically serves as the main frame of reference for relative value, along with any other visible and relevant data points from private-placement transactions.

Similar to the project loan market, the spreads on project finance bonds tightened significantly during the 2005–2007 credit boom to roughly +100 bps to +200 bps. After the global financial crisis, they widened to +200 bps to +300 bps. The regulatory tightening in the post-crisis period seems to have had a smaller effect on bonds than on bank loans.

10.5 Project and Infrastructure Debt Market Evolution

Although the supply of project financings showed few signs of slowing in the aftermath of the global financial crisis, the availability of adequate debt financing remained uncertain. Post-crisis regulatory changes affecting the global banking system in combination with bank lending's critical role at the front end of project financing clouded the outlook for infrastructure financing.

The Bank for International Settlements (BIS) Basel III mandates, as well as tougher annual stress-testing rules in many countries, have forced banks to deleverage in order to shore up their loss-bearing capital and increase their balance sheets' liquidity, with target ratios prescribed for both credit and liquidity risk exposures. In response to these new regulations, many banks (particularly those domiciled in Europe) have scaled back their long-term lending exposures to existing and new illiquid assets such as project loans. Moreover, because most project financings have been US dollar-based, project lending volumes were further dampened (at least initially) by key European banks' constrained access to US dollar funding.

To plug the funding gap created by bank lenders backing away from the project finance market, infrastructure funds and sovereign wealth funds have begun to look at investments in project finance debt, mainly the more junior portions of projects' capital structure (as opposed to senior secured bank loans). Multilateral and government efforts have also aimed to expand the institutional investor base for project and infrastructure bonds.

One supranational example is the Europe 2020 Project Bond Initiative, a joint effort between the European Commission and the European Investment Bank (EIB). As part of this initiative the EIB provides credit enhancement through a subordinated instrument (either a loan or contingent backstop facility) to bolster demand from insurance companies and pension funds for senior bonds issued to finance approved European infrastructure projects (typically PPP structures).

Another country-level example comes from the Reserve Bank of India, which in 2013 approved the regulatory framework for a system of Infrastructure Debt Funds (IDFs). These funds can borrow from domestic and international insurance companies as well as pension funds to finance investments in domestic PPP projects.

Still, no magic bullet has materialized to meet the vast prospective demand for financing infrastructure projects. The project finance market has been searching for a solution to the problem created by retreating banks — namely, finding new sources of debt capital. For this reason, the project finance debt market remains one of the few credit markets where pricing has not yet returned to pre-crisis levels.

11. Establishing Robust Markets for Infrastructure-backed Securities

In addition to capital raising through bank lending and primary bond and stock offerings, a robust global financial architecture must provide the opportunity for institutional investors to shift portfolio profiles easily, quickly, and cheaply in the face of change. Such changes include interest rate expectations, risk perceptions, comparative returns, and other aspects of the portfolio optimization search. And because most institutional investors are fiduciaries, they are obliged to act in their beneficiaries' interests — that is, institutional investors are subject to both "duty of care" and "duty of loyalty" to their clients.

The exercise of fund management obligations may be made more difficult in the case of infrastructure financings because of the nature of the financial instruments that emanate from them. This may be a key bottleneck for financial efficiency in the infrastructure "air supply" mentioned earlier. Consequently, the focus has to be on the efficiency of both the primary and secondary markets for debt instruments generated by project and infrastructure financings.

11.1 Primary Markets for Infrastructure-backed Securities

A "primary" market for a security provides pricing and transfer of ownership from the issuer to the initial holders. A "secondary" market allows for subsequent purchases and sales that do not involve the issuer. Assuming that an infrastructure-backed security (IBS) will closely resemble traditional debt and equity securities, we can sketch out how these markets might operate.

The primary market needs to be structured so as to encourage private production of information and competition among potential investors. Information production is necessary because IBS valuation will require specialized knowledge given the underlying projects' scale and complexity, even under the most thorough and transparent disclosure regimes. Vigorous competition among investors, transparency, and market discipline will presumably address these concerns for purely private-sector issues. Even with public-sector issues, competition is necessary because the governments likely to be the securities' primary guarantors need to convince their diverse political constituencies that the project is not a "giveaway" to wealthy and well-connected investors.

The two standard frameworks for primary markets are *auctions* and *underwriting syndicates*.

Auctions (such as the "modified Dutch auction" used in Google's 2004 IPO, or the primary dealer-based auctions used for US Treasury securities) are generally viewed as transparent, fair, and competitive. Competition in auctions, however, depends on high participation (many bidders) as well as measures to discourage collusion. The record of electromagnetic spectrum auctions, which can be viewed as large direct transfers of infrastructure ownership, has been notably flawed in this regard.[1]

Moreover, even though some observers expected Google's IPO to validate the auction format and lead to widespread adoption of auction procedures, the number of equity IPO auctions has not seen strong growth. Research has suggested that the high efficiency generally associated with auctions actually allows too much free-riding on the costly production of private information. This argument can be used to justify the conventional IPO underwriting process, despite its high cost in terms of fees and persistent underpricing.

In most countries today, *underwriting syndicates* remain the dominant primary market mechanism for issuing risky securities.[2] Because

---

1   See Binmore and Klemperer (2002) and Klemperer (2002a, 2002b).
2   See Sherman (2005) and Chiang, Qian, and Sherman (2010).

production of private information is likely to be a key element of the infrastructure-backed securities origination process in the debt capital markets, similar considerations will likely apply to this sector as well.

11.2 Secondary Markets for Infrastructure-backed Securities

Although a viable secondary market is not strictly essential for infrastructure finance, future opportunities for IBS resale can increase the securities' value in the primary market, which will reduce borrowing rates and therefore the cost of capital.

IBS are inherently long-term securities, as discussed earlier — longer than the investment horizons of all big asset pools except perhaps endowment funds and multi-generation family offices. IBS are also undiversified. Both of these dimensions suggest strong non-informational reasons for secondary-market trading.

The most liquid secondary markets are for equities, and these are generally organized as electronic "limit order books". Using this mechanism, traders enter buy and sell orders with limit prices. If a new incoming buy order's limit price meets or exceeds the lowest price of the previously entered sell orders (the "ask book"), the orders are matched and a trade occurs. If the incoming buy order cannot be matched against any sell order in the ask book, it is added to the bid book, where it will be available for matching against newly arriving sell orders.

In the more widely used "lit" form of this market, the bid and ask books are visible and widely disseminated; in a "dark" market, bids and asks are not displayed. Because orders are handled continuously on a first-come, first-served basis, faster traders have an advantage over slower ones, which has given rise to the practice of automated high-frequency trading. The electronic limit order markets feature high transparency and are readily accessible by retail and institutional investors. This form of market organization dominates in equities and standardized futures and options contracts.

These markets usually function well when there is sufficient natural trading interest, which is often associated with dispersed ownership and inclusion of the securities in an index or exchange-traded funds

(ETFs). They sometimes require assistance, however, from designated market makers (DMMs) and auctions. DMMs assume the responsibility of ensuring that there is always a posted bid and offer during regular continuous trading sessions. When natural trading interest is too low to warrant operation of a continuous market, once-a-day "double auctions" are often used.

Existing debt securities, such as bonds and notes, generally trade in *dealer markets*. These markets rely on intermediaries that take the other side of customer trades. Banks have traditionally performed this function. After the global financial crisis and application "Volcker Rule" as part of the US Dodd-Frank legislation, however, bans on proprietary trading have limited banks' dealing capabilities. This limitation creates an opening for other players (e.g., hedge funds) that are willing to commit capital and develop expertise in the securities and markets concerned.[3]

The quality of dealer markets in debt securities varies widely. They are generally viewed as adequately serving institutional trading needs for corporate and sovereign bonds. They are less successful in providing trading opportunities for retail investors. In contrast to equity markets, proportional trading costs are lower for larger institutional trades than smaller retail trades.

For IBS, although the amount of capital raised in the retail sector might be small, the possibility of some local retail participation could help sustain consensus in the political sphere. Even at their best, dealer markets tend to suffer from low transparency.

In some respects, infrastructure-backed debt securities may most closely resemble the existing municipal bond market in the US. This market segment includes debt that is often issued to build public infrastructure or, as in the case of IRBs, private infrastructure that serves an identifiable public purpose.

The current municipal bond market does not provide a desirable template or starting point for an infrastructure finance architecture. It is extremely fragmented. The Mergent Online database lists about 3.6 million issues of municipal securities, roughly 10 times the number of US corporate debt issues. Trading costs are high. Sirri (2014) finds that

---

3   Whitehead (2011).

the median customer-to-customer differential (similar to the bid-ask spread) is 198 bps. The average differential for retail-sized trades (up to $5,000) is 246 bps.

The US municipal bond market therefore provides a cautionary model for IBS debt. In most cases, this model would be hampered by the absence of the interest tax subsidy that exists for municipal debt in the US.

Finally, as noted earlier, the vast bulk of debt issued by municipalities and IRBs has final maturities of less than 10 years, whereas the financial time-profile of optimal debt for infrastructure projects often significantly exceeds that maturity. This dynamic suggests an extraordinary opportunity for improving capital market access for infrastructure projects by creating new ways of generating liquidity for investors.

12. Infrastructure Equity as an Asset Class

With many large publicly listed companies, index funds, and ETFs, infrastructure has recently established itself as a new investable asset class for institutional and retail equity investors. Likewise, private equity funds have raised many billions of dollars from institutions and high-net-worth individuals to deploy in infrastructure financings.

One driver of the surge in interest has been a "great rotation" out of standard fixed-income products into investments that are less sensitive to rising interest rates yet deliver "bond-like" cash flows.

But are infrastructure investments more like bonds or more like stocks? Here we look at the risk and return of listed infrastructure assets. We consider three listed infrastructure indexes:

1. MSCI World Core Infrastructure Index (WCII)

2. MSCI World Infrastructure Index (WII)

3. MSCI Emerging Markets Infrastructure Index (EMII)[1]

We next detail their composition. Complicating the analysis, the sample periods are not only short but also characterized by the most serious financial crisis in several generations during 2007–2009. The longer sample additionally includes the technology boom and bust of 1999 through 2001 as well as the aftermath of late-1990s Asian Financial Crisis.

---

1   The WCII is available only from December 2003 onward (138 months). WII and EMII have data from January 1999 onward (197 months).

We compare infrastructure equity's performance against that of (1) the MSCI World Core Real Estate Index (CREI), which invests in listed companies that own and operate commercial real estate worldwide; (2) global stocks (the world market portfolio from Kenneth French's data library);[2] and (3) global bonds (the Barclays Aggregate Bond Index).[3]

Table 4 shows the summary statistics. For the full sample period from 1999 through 2015, the WII performed quite poorly, with an average annual return of 4.0%, annual volatility of 14.4%, and an annual Sharpe ratio of only 0.14.[4] For comparison, global stocks as a whole had average returns of 6.9% with 15.7% volatility, implying a Sharpe ratio more than twice as high as for infrastructure.

A good deal of this poor performance occurred between 1999 and 2002, when stocks performed quite poorly as well. In sharp contrast, the EMII had much higher returns of 10.4% per year over the full sample, albeit with higher volatility of 20.7%. This performance is almost as good as real estate, which logs the highest return and the highest Sharpe ratio among all asset classes during the 16.5 years covered by the data.[5]

In the shorter 2003–2015 subsample (Panel B), the WII recorded much higher average returns of 9.0% per year. The annual volatility was 12.7%, and the annual Sharpe ratio was an impressive 0.61. Both the WCII and the EMII performed even better, however, with annual returns of 12.1% and 12.7% and volatilities of 13.4% and 18.4%. The WCII has an impressive Sharpe ratio of 0.80. For comparison, global stocks recorded 9.1% average annual returns with 15.5% volatility, and global real estate stocks had average returns of 11.0% but with a much higher volatility of 20.5%.

The reason the WCII outperformed the WII comes from the comparatively strong returns in the transportation sub-sector (which the WCII overweights) and weaker returns in telecommunications infrastructure (which the WCII underweights). The low volatility of

---

2   Available at http://mba.tuck.dartmouth.edu/pages/faculty/ken.french/data_library. html

3   Available at http://etfdb.com/index/barclays-capital-global-aggregate-bond-index

4   The Sharpe ratio measures an investment's performance by adjusting for its risk — *the excess return (or risk premium)* per unit of deviation in an investment asset.

5   Both infrastructure indices have negative skewness, although not as much as stocks or real estate. Skewness measures the asymmetry of the *probability distribution* of a real-valued *random variable* around its mean.

infrastructure is noteworthy, especially in light of the financial crisis, which weighs heavily on this short sample period.

Table 4. Comparative Infrastructure Returns — Summary
Statistics (Source: own calculations)

Panel A: January 1999–June 2015						
	WCII	WII	EMII	CREI	Stocks	Bonds
Mean		4.0	10.4	10.8	6.9	4.3
Std. Dev.		14.4	20.7	18.4	15.7	5.7
Sharpe		0.14	0.41	0.48	0.32	0.41
Skew		−0.51	−0.34	−1.07	−0.73	0.05
Panel B: December 2003–June 2015						
	WCII	WII	EMII	CREI	Stocks	Bonds
Mean	12.1	9.0	12.7	11.0	9.1	4.0
Std. Dev.	13.4	12.7	18.4	20.5	15.5	5.7
Sharpe	0.80	0.61	0.62	0.47	0.50	0.47
Skew	−0.99	−0.80	−0.80	−1.09	−0.94	−0.10

The next question is whether listed infrastructure stocks and bonds perform similarly. To address this question, we estimate a regression of the excess return on the infrastructure indexes against the excess return on global stocks, the excess return on global bonds, and a constant. Table 5 presents the results.

For the full sample, we find that about 70% of variation in both the WII and EMII returns is accounted for by global stock and bond returns. The WII has a stock beta of 0.73 and a bond beta of 0.24. The EMII has a much higher stock beta of 1.08 and a lower bond beta of 0.07.

For the shorter sample, stocks and bonds explain 70% to 75% of return variation in the WII and EMII, and even 85% of variation in the WCII. The WII stock beta falls to 0.61 and its bond beta rises to 0.47. The WCII stock beta is 0.69 and its bond beta is 0.52. The EMII has the highest stock beta (0.91) and the lowest bond beta (0.45).

We conclude that exposure to two risk factors, global stock and bond market risk, goes a long way toward explaining the observed returns on the various infrastructure indexes.

Infrastructure investment is much more stock-like than bond-like, particularly for emerging markets infrastructure. This important finding may help define the boundaries of the investor community as well as pools of capital that may be available for infrastructure finance.

Table 5. Risk Characteristics of Infrastructure
(Source: own calculations)

	Panel A: 1999–2015		Panel B: 2003–2015		
	WII	EMII	WCII	WII	EMII
alpha	−0.18	0.24	0.33	0.13	0.26
	−1.1	0.9	2.4	0.9	1.0
stock beta	0.73	1.08	0.69	0.61	0.91
	14.0	20.7	19.2	11.9	15.9
bond beta	0.24	0.07	0.52	0.47	0.45
	2.0	0.5	4.9	3.5	2.8
R2	68.7	68.8	85.5	75.6	70.5
Exp. Return	6.1	7.5	8.8	7.4	9.6

We also note that the EMII's and WCII's performance are not only stellar in absolute return terms but also strong in risk-adjusted terms. We address this issue in terms of *alpha*, which measures the monthly abnormal return of an asset or portfolio of assets after accounting for global stock and bond risk.

Based on our dataset, EMII had a 0.24% per month or 2.9% per year return in excess of what would be justified based on its risk (see the last row of Table 5). So, rather than generating a 7.5% return, it generated 2.9% more for a total return of 10.4%. For the shorter sample, the WCII even outperformed the index by 33 bps per month.[6] Core Infrastructure delivered 4.0% more return than the required rate of return of 8.1%.

With this cost of capital in hand, we can make sense of current valuation ratios on listed infrastructure equities.

Figure 4 plots the price-dividend ratios on the three indexes. Infrastructure assets were very expensive during the 1999–2000 period,

---

6   The alpha is statistically significant at the 5% level despite the short sample.

probably because of a combination of the euphoria in stock markets and the novelty of the infrastructure asset class. Valuation ratios fell by half in the ensuing stock market crash. Valuations rebounded in the mid-2000s, only to crash again during the 2007–2008 financial crisis. Since 2009, they have rebounded strongly. At the end of our sample in May 2015, Core Infrastructure traded at a price-dividend ratio of 31.25, Emerging Market Infrastructure at 27.4, and the WII at 26.3.

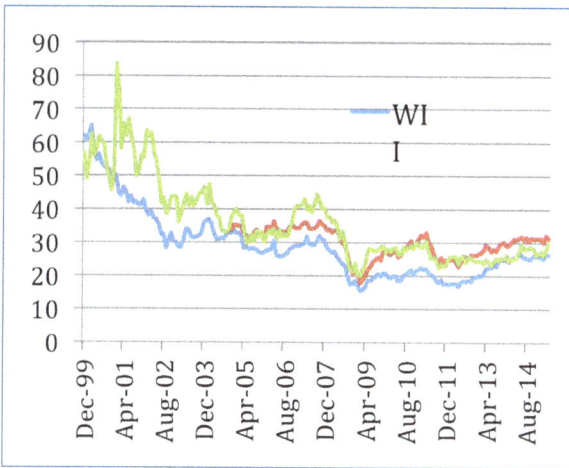

Figure 4. Price-Dividend Ratios on Infrastructure Indices (Source: own calculations)

Given its good fit, we take the expected return given by the global two-factor model as a good measure of the required rate of return to discount future cash flows. The question then becomes, what dividend growth rates do the current valuations imply? We focus on the WCII for the 2004–2015 sample period.

Dividend growth on the WCII averaged 7.25% per year. If that growth rate were to continue this pace, the WCII should trade for a price-dividend ratio double the level we observed in May 2015. Under a more conservative scenario that dividend growth will remain high in 2015 (10%) and then fall by 1% every year until it hits a long-term mean growth rate of 4.15% in 2021 and beyond, the price is right. Given the strong need for global infrastructure, this set of growth forecasts seems eminently reasonable.

In sum, after a rocky start in the late 1990s and early 2000s, infrastructure performed remarkably well as an asset class during the past decade. Despite the strong rise in prices of listed infrastructure assets since the depth of the financial crisis, infrastructure assets remained attractively valued, especially in light of the very high cash flow growth rates in the recent past. Such high cash-flow growth is predicted to continue in the short term but eventually to mean-revert to lower levels.

13. Project and Infrastructure Debt as an Asset Class

The credit rating agencies, notably Standard & Poor's, have been active in analyzing project and infrastructure-based bond debt from the perspective of default risk.[1] Figure 5 shows project and infrastructure finance ratings from 1982 to 2004.

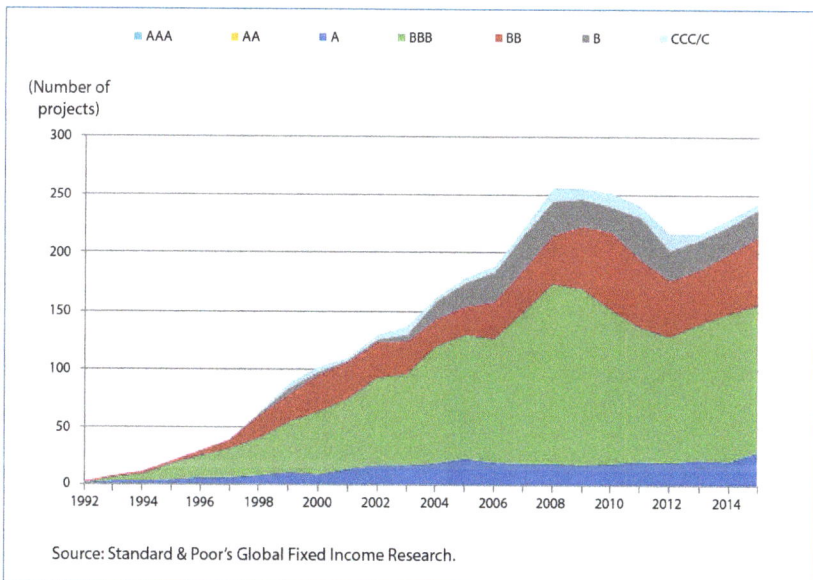

Figure 5. Historical Project Finance Ratings Outstanding, 1992–2014
(Source: © Standard & Poor, 2015)

---

1   2014 Project Finance Default Study and Rating Transitions, Standard & Poor's Ratings Direct, 23 February 2016.

As of the end of 2015, there were about 250 S&P-rated infrastructure issues, the majority of which are rated BBB, the lowest investment grade, and therefore acceptable in key institutional portfolios. Issues rated as A presumably are backed by highly rated sponsors and therefore do not qualify as non-recourse project financing. The remaining infrastructure bond issues are non-investment "speculative" grade. Figure 6 shows the distribution by geography and rating, and Figure 7 shows the distribution by sector and rating.

Note the dominance of investment-grade ratings in the OECD countries, with a significant Latin American representation. Infrastructure among the rated sectorial projects is dominated by power, transportation, and public finance/real estate. Note the marginal role of telecommunications among project-based rated debt issues. The power sector, in turn, is highly sensitive to risk-shifting contracts such as offtake contracts with strong counterparties and significant liquidity providers in place.

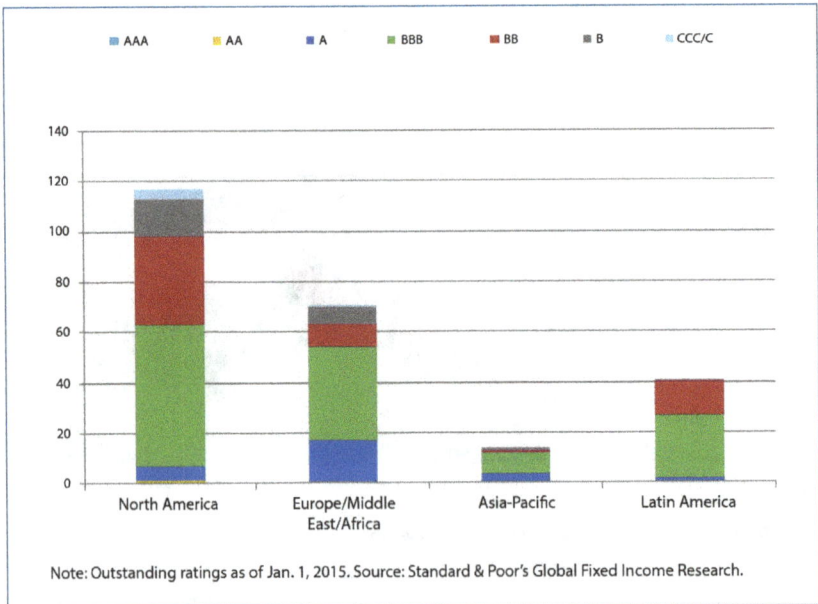

Note: Outstanding ratings as of Jan. 1, 2015. Source: Standard & Poor's Global Fixed Income Research.

Figure 6. Project Finance Ratings by Region
(Source: © Standard & Poor, 2015)

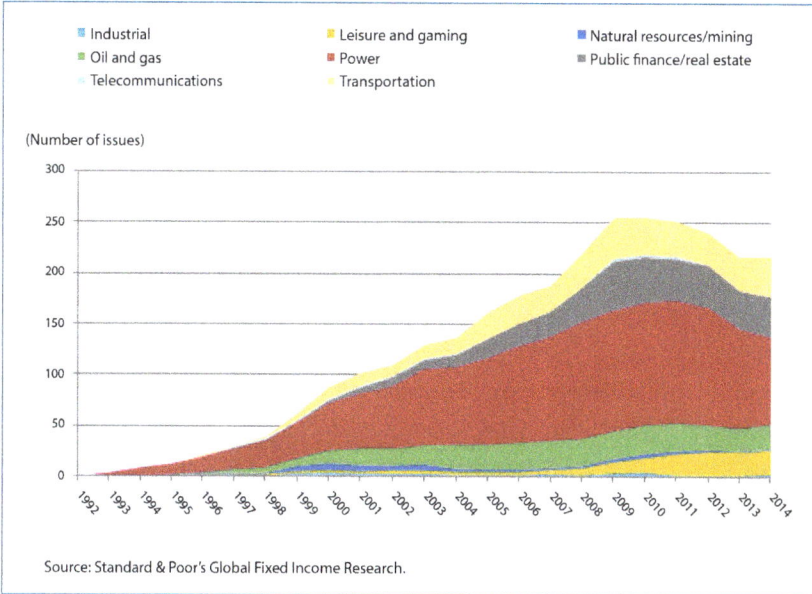

Figure 7. Historical Project Finance Ratings by Industry
(Source: © Standard & Poor, 2015)

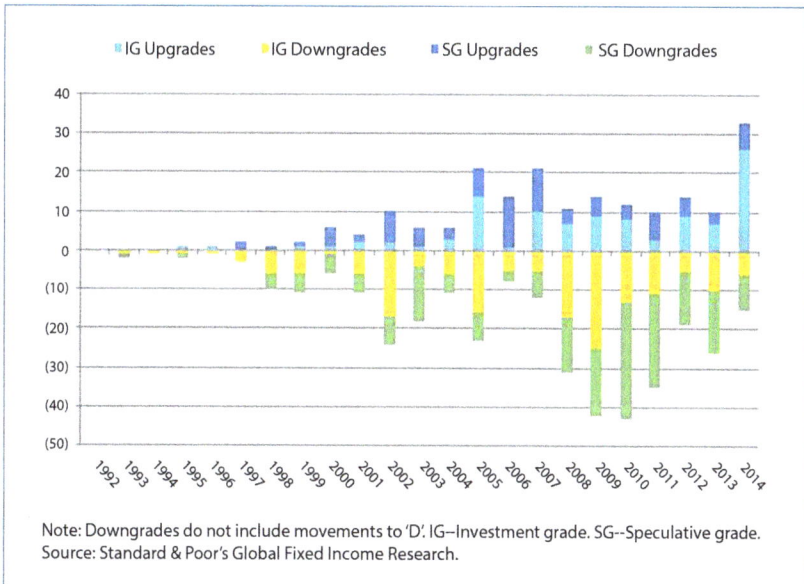

Figure 8. Annual Project Finance Ratings Actions
(Source: © Standard & Poor, 2015)

How stable are the ratings? Figure 8 shows ratings upgrades and downgrades of investment-grade and speculative issues, respectively, in the project finance arena, evidently with significant re-rating activity during the 1982–1994 period. It shows a higher share of upgrades toward the end of the period, notably in the power sector. Re-ratings are reflected in transition matrixes, showing ratings migration over periods from one to five years after issue. As expected, ratings migration is highest in the lower investment-grade and speculative-grade project and infrastructure securities.

Table 6 shows cumulative default rates for infrastructure issues, by rating, for different time periods since issue. For BBB issues the cumulative default rate was 4.3% over 15 years, and for speculative issues it was 20.1% for the same period.[2] Overall, 5.8% of the S&P project population defaulted, and 68% of these had an initial speculative-grade rating with a median rating of BB.

Table 6. Cumulative Average Default Rates (%) for Project Finance Issues (Source: © Standard & Poor, 2015)

Cumulative Average Default Rates (%)														
						--Time horizon (years)--								
Rating	1	2	3	4	5	6	7	8	9	10	11	12	13	14	15
AAA	0.00	0.00	0.00	0.00	0.00	0.00	0.00	0.00	0.00	0.00	0.00	0.00	0.00	0.00	0.00
AA	0.00	0.00	0.00	0.00	0.00	0.00	0.00	0.00	0.00	0.00	0.00	0.00	0.00	0.00	0.00
A	0.00	0.00	0.35	0.73	1.14	1.59	2.09	2.63	2.63	2.63	2.63	2.63	2.63	2.63	2.63
BBB	0.23	0.47	0.67	0.96	1.27	1.36	1.56	1.79	2.07	2.57	3.16	3.89	4.79	4.79	4.79
BB	0.61	1.93	4.98	7.34	9.13	10.17	11.08	12.12	13.31	13.76	14.26	14.83	15.51	16.36	17.47
B	3.30	8.69	11.48	14.61	16.73	17.34	18.03	18.89	20.03	21.77	21.77	21.77	21.77	21.77	21.77
CCC/C	18.10	24.09	27.25	28.46	29.84	29.84	29.84	29.84	29.84	29.84	29.84	29.84	29.84	29.84	29.84
Investment grade	0.19	0.40	0.62	0.92	1.24	1.39	1.63	1.92	2.15	2.54	3.01	3.59	4.30	4.30	4.30
Speculative grade	3.10	6.05	9.04	11.50	13.33	14.15	14.91	15.80	16.86	17.50	17.88	18.33	18.89	19.59	20.51

Evidence from the rated project finance market relies on a small share of the thousands of project financings done every year, so these data do not represent the market as a whole. Moreover, the dataset breakdown has some bond tranches too small to permit meaningful conclusions. Nevertheless, if the future of infrastructure finance is to tap the world's large fiduciary asset pools, it must demonstrate a growing trend toward

---

2   *Ibid.*

investment-grade issues, which the data currently indicate. There are also interregional differences — for example, speculative-grade project finance captures 46% of the activity in North America but only 24% in Europe.

Finally, in recent years financing mechanisms and funds invested in sustainable infrastructure have grown exponentially.

Green bonds, for example, have grown from $10 billion in 2013 to $45 billion in 2015. At the international level, global commitments by governments toward a low-carbon future, in conjunction with the UN SDGs, have led to multilateral banks such as the World Bank and the Asia Development Bank working to de-risk private-sector investment in sustainable infrastructure by leveraging their AAA rating to issue social impact bonds. A Green Climate Fund has been set up to assist with the climate commitments, and governments around the world have committed $100 billion to stimulate the transition to a low-carbon economy.

At the national, state, and municipal level, PPPs are emerging to tackle water infrastructure issues, among other needs. In the US, Connecticut and New York have set up "green banks" focused on catalyzing investment in renewable energy and water quality infrastructure.

The US EPA launched its Water Infrastructure and Resiliency Finance Center in January 2015, which incorporates a Clean Water State Revolving Fund and a Drinking Water State Revolving Fund aimed at financing resilient water infrastructure as well as storm-water and green infrastructure programs. The funds do not depend on Congressional appropriations. They make loans, purchase debt obligations, securitize financing, provide guarantees, and carry an AAA rating. Annual new issues have been around $2 billion, with the projected need rising to $3 billion to $4 billion annually.

The Chinese government has set up a formal process for infrastructure PPPs as part of its goal to bring more private-sector financing to address environmental challenges, many of which are infrastructure related.

One apparent trend is growing demand from institutional investors and smaller "impact investors" for fixed-income, long-term investments that create social benefit. Securitization of green infrastructure, such as energy-efficiency loans and solar power, are beginning to create a more liquid secondary market for infrastructure improvements.

14. Portfolio Optimization: Institutional Investors and Asset Managers

The foregoing risk and return analysis for infrastructure equity has direct implications for institutions and individuals seeking to invest in infrastructure as an asset class.

Here we focus on the 2003–2015 period and consider a large institutional investor such as a major pension fund that seeks to combine global stocks, bonds, real estate, and infrastructure in an optimal portfolio.

To make the problem more realistic in light of observed institutional portfolios, we impose maximum weights of 45% in bonds, 15% in real estate, and 15% in infrastructure.

Using the WCII definition, the minimum-variance portfolio holds the maximum 15% in infrastructure and 45% in bonds. It holds 36% in stocks and 4% in real estate. This portfolio has the same return as a 65%/35% stock/bond portfolio but has lower volatility and therefore a much higher Sharpe ratio: 0.62 versus 0.54.

The bottom line is that the historical data provide a compelling rationale for shifting traditional stock/bond portfolios toward real estate and infrastructure. Doing so in a way that maintains return and increases Sharpe ratio requires reducing the stock position and increasing the bond position.

It appears that institutional investors such as sovereign wealth funds, pension funds, insurance companies, and endowments do in fact tend to allocate similar fractions to real estate and infrastructure.

One study[1] reports an average target allocation to real estate of 9.4% in 2014 (up 0.5% bps from 2013), with an intention to increase this allocation to 9.6% during 2015. The average fraction actually invested is only slightly lower, at 8.5%. These weights are close to real estate's weight in the world market portfolio of investable assets.

The findings for Infrastructure are similar. Preqin[2] reports that average allocation to infrastructure for institutional investors increased from 3.5% of AUM in 2011 to 4.3% in 2015. Target allocations to this asset class continued to grow in 2015 and stood at 6.3% of AUM in mid-2016 for those investors allocating to the asset class. Preqin also reports that allocations to infrastructure are likely to continue to grow in the coming years, with 44% of investors planning to increase the amount of capital they invest in the asset class.

---

1   See Funk, Weill, and Hodes (2014).
2   See https://www.preqin.com

15. Accelerating Infrastructure Finance

This study is intended as an up-to-date discussion of the global issue of infrastructure finance, starting with the fundamentals of infrastructure development and ending with concrete questions about tapping global pools of investable funds. We take as given the enormous financial requirements presented by the infrastructure sector in the years ahead, as well as the equally enormous pools of investable funds in perennial search of optimal portfolio allocation.

The core question is how to better connect the requirements and the resources in a mutually advantageous way — the disciplined identification of viable and sustainable infrastructure initiatives on the one hand, and the equally disciplined risk, liquidity, and return attributes on the other. We suggest that this is decisively a positive-sum game, with impressive gains for both sides and, in most cases, equally impressive spillovers for society more generally.

15.1 Recap

We began this study by defining the boundaries for the kinds of capital investments properly termed "infrastructure". We continued with the attributes of infrastructure activities that distinguish them from other economic activities. These features include scale, capital-intensity, longevity, and generation of public benefits that can be difficult to value and internalize for purposes of creating viable financial structures.

We next outlined key complexities in a section on the legal dimensions of infrastructure projects, including governing law and the use of eminent domain.

All of these elements add to the underlying complexity of infrastructure finance. Each needs to be documented, priced, stress-tested across contingencies, and built into financial contracts that become the basis of financial instruments that fit investor portfolios.

Perhaps even more problematic are the political, environmental, and social issues related to infrastructure development, whether or not anchored in legal documentation. These attributes and the associated political risks accompany all infrastructure projects, affect their cost and revenue characteristics, and sometimes block them altogether.

Infrastructure finance investors try to address such issues by creating risk parameters reflected in their investment decision criteria as well as in the contractual design of infrastructure projects.

Following the generic framework of infrastructure projects, we went on to consider the global infrastructure industry's industrial organization — its structure, conduct, and performance — to demonstrate the importance of competition in the infrastructure-development industry, including the role of concessionary finance.

Measuring the depth of globalization in this industry sector is complicated because of differences in how infrastructure is defined, different modes of participation (e.g., project financing, equipment supply, design, construction, and operation), and the fact that large projects often involve consortia with participants from diverse countries. The role of Chinese firms in the global infrastructure industry deserved special mention in this discussion.

We turned next to the development, character, complexities, and risks of infrastructure finance — one of the most challenging activities in all of global finance.

On the project side, we discussed the economic viability essentials for investors to review that incorporate a defensible assessment of risk attributes — both project risks themselves and the risk mitigation structures that surround them. We discussed project life cycles and the role of various forms of financing, from bank lending and sponsor equity to long-term fixed-income securities. On the investor side, we discussed how project finance fits into institutional portfolios managed by pension funds, insurance companies, hedge funds, and other large asset pools in terms of returns, risks, and liquidity.

Liquidity was considered separately as a key issue, particularly with respect to gaps in current market microstructures that do not perform well in providing liquidity for the long maturities involved in infrastructure finance. Financial innovation may in the future create infrastructure-related obligations with improved liquidity properties, which could make institutional investors much more receptive to infrastructure bonds.

As we emphasized in our empirical discussion of returns and risks associated with infrastructure finance as an asset class, the picture for investors is encouraging. This was true even during the extreme financial turbulence of the global financial crisis. We examined whether infrastructure-linked securities are more like bonds or more like stocks in the asset allocation of major institutional investors such as pension funds and life insurance companies — asset managers that seek to combine global stocks, bonds, real estate, and infrastructure in what they view as optimal portfolios.

We then calibrated performance of the infrastructure asset classes from 2003 through 2015. We found that infrastructure financing is highly correlated with stocks and bonds but exhibits much higher returns than the relevant combination of stocks and bonds alone. These results suggest that infrastructure finance can indeed form a robust asset class in institutional investors' portfolios worldwide. So what is next?

15.2 There Is No Alternative to Robust Debt Markets

Project finance will inevitably be central to meeting the world's infrastructure needs in both developing and developed countries, given the very long-term nature of infrastructure assets and the multiplicity of risks involved. We have emphasized in this study that project finance allows sponsors — whether corporations, governments, or financial sponsors such as private equity funds — to maximize the amount of debt in infrastructure initiatives' capital structure, typically up to 70%

to 80%. So the dynamics of the global debt markets are central to the whole discussion.

Institutional investment funds in the pension and insurance sectors alone are estimated to have managed more than $50 trillion in 2015, but only 0.8% of these assets were invested in infrastructure projects worldwide.[1] Given infrastructure debt's built-in inflation protection, stable returns, high recovery rates, and low correlations with other asset classes, the global market for it should be much larger among the world's growing long-term investment pools than it is today. Whereas the construction phase, particularly in greenfield projects, will likely continue to rely on banking expertise and bank lending as the form of finance, it seems logical that securitized bank debt and bonds covering the operating phase of infrastructure projects should be well suited for the key institutional investors.

For a high-leverage approach to work in this context, the debt emanating from infrastructure projects must be available in ample supply, and the average debt cost must be kept low — in today's market, usually in the mid-single-digit coupon range. Low debt costs imply the need for investment-grade credit ratings for most project finance debt.

15.3 Banking Pressures

The first impediment to improved bridging of sources and uses of infrastructure debt comes from commercial banks. As noted, these banks dominate the project finance debt market and are particularly important in the pre-completion phase. Overall, commercial banks provide roughly 90% to 95% of total project debt in any given year.

Because commercial banks earn significant up-front fees for structuring and advising on projects, they are often willing to lend at fairly thin margins, sometimes in the low single-digit (2% to 3% yield) range. Attractive debt cost is compelling for borrowers, as is the ability to negotiate with a small group of relationship lenders, particularly during the critical project construction period. Consequently, most project and infrastructure finance sponsors have little incentive to refinance bank

---

1   [n.a.], "A Long and Winding Road". *The Economist*. 22 March, 2014

debt with project bonds, even when a project begins generating cash flow, unless the lending banks face balance sheet capacity issues.

The progressive implementation of the Basel III banking regulations under the auspices of the Bank for International Settlements (BIS) affected the conditions in the project finance debt market. The thinking was that the new minimum capital and liquidity ratios would prevent commercial banks (particularly European banks) from holding illiquid long-term project finance loans on their balance sheets. Indeed, almost 10 years after the financial crisis, key European banks continue to wrestle with capital adequacy resulting from their failure to raise capital soon after the financial turbulence. So these banks presumably would be sensitive today to holding risky long-term assets on their balance sheets and less willing to finance up to 90% of project debt, forcing sponsors to inject more equity.

Perhaps surprisingly, the European project finance banks seem to have adjusted to the Basel III regulations fairly smoothly and without materially throttling infrastructure project lending.

Despite some reallocation of market share among the major project lending banks — notably, the Japanese banks have become more aggressive — there has been no noticeable decline in overall new project lending volumes, no forced secondary sales of on-balance-sheet loans, and no meaningful increase in project bond refinancings during the past few years. Moreover, because project loans have relatively high average credit quality, low default rates, and high recovery rates compared with loans in most other sectors, project loans arguably remain a better use of bank balance sheet capacity than some alternatives.

At the same time, the investment-grade bond market is very well suited to project and infrastructure financing.

- The market is very large ($5.4 trillion outstanding at market prices as of December 31, 2015).[2]

- It is long-dated (10.4 years average maturity) and global in nature.

- It is well versed in analyzing cross-border sovereign risk.

---

2   Barclays Bank at https://www.barclayscorporate.com/products-and-solutions/financing/corporate-lending/infrastructure-and-project-finance.html

- It is low cost (3.00% to 4.00% average yield-to-worst for all issues).

- It is dominated by institutional investors such as life insurance companies and pension funds, which typically prefer long-dated bonds to match their long-term liabilities.

In short, the global high-grade bond market seems to be an ideal arena to generate the large amounts of debt capital required to finance projected infrastructure needs. So far, however, it has been significantly underutilized.

The investment-grade bond market appears optimal for most project finance bonds, particularly in a continued environment of extremely low interest rates and scarcity of new public bond issuance following a period of heavy corporate refinancing. However, the market has issued only $25 billion to $50 billion per year from 2003 through 2015. The run-rate of investment grade project and infrastructure bonds appears minimal, and it should be possible to materially expand it.

15.4 Infrastructure Finance Expertise

A second infrastructure finance bottleneck lies with the specific skill-sets involved in analyzing and pricing project finance bonds. The complex financial and nonfinancial risks discussed earlier, the document-intensive nature of project finance structures, and the variety of legal contracts and bond covenants built into most such financings demand a high level of analytical skill.

The analysis required is more typical of the high-yield bond market than of the investment-grade bond arena. Nevertheless, a small community of investment-grade bond investors has developed expertise in this area. Most project finance bond offerings to date have been bought by a handful of large insurance companies with private placement groups, such as MetLife, John Hancock, Travelers, and AIG in the US.

A number of global asset management firms including BlackRock, JPMorgan Asset Management, and Allianz SE have built investment teams with project finance expertise and raised funds to invest in project and infrastructure loans and bonds. The bulk of these funds come from second-tier and smaller insurance companies as well as pension funds that lack the in-house capacity to analyze such debt.

Moreover, some of the aforementioned insurance companies have also raised third-party funds to invest in project debt, marketed on the back of their private placement franchises.

Such capital-raising moves were geared to take advantage of expected changes in the project finance bank debt market resulting from the application of Basel III rules. As noted earlier, these changes did not play out quite as expected. The end result is that much of this newly raised capital has not yet been deployed because of a worldwide scarcity of viable project and infrastructure finance deals, while pricing on closed project debt financings has tightened in response to increased competition.

15.5 Liquidity Issues

The third major obstacle to project and infrastructure financing growth through the global investment-grade bond markets is liquidity.

Most project finance bonds issued to date have been in traditional private placement format, with limited secondary market trading once a new issue is placed with institutional investors. Typically, most insurance companies would not opt to sell a project finance bond unless a credit event resulted in a downgrade of the issuer below investment grade.

Compared to classic private placements, using the more-liquid US Rule 144A private placement format, which allows reselling bonds to "qualified institutional buyers" and opens project and infrastructure finance bonds to a wider universe of potential buyers, assuming the investing institutions have the requisite analytical skills.

So far, most 144A project finance issues have been dominated by traditional private placement life insurance-industry investors. If the volume of 144A project finance bonds were to increase significantly, it is safe to assume that other institutional investors would opt to build their in-house capacity to research and trade these securities as opposed to outsourcing this function for a management fee — this would effectively help disintermediate the aforementioned asset management firms.

Improved secondary market liquidity would also help facilitate broader trading interest in investment-grade project and infrastructure finance bonds. At present, only three or four Wall Street firms actively trade project finance debt,[3] although the number of market makers arguably will increase in line with greater new-issuance volumes. Increasing secondary-market price transparency would also help facilitate more of a two-way aftermarket.[4]

Another step to expand the universe of project finance bonds is accessing the upper end of the US high-yield ("junk") bond market, although this market is limited in tenor (7 to 10 years) and provincial in its credit focus (only domestic issuers, including US independent power producers and liquefied natural gas project developers). Moreover, in a rising interest rate environment, the economics of issuing high-yield project finance bonds, even those rated BB, may be problematic.

Lastly, discussions around developing a liquid, index-type project finance bond structure using CDO-style architecture have not yet led anywhere. Nonetheless, the concept of using a portfolio approach to project finance bond issuance clearly has merit, because it would diversify overall cash flows and improve market receptivity for infrastructure-related bonds.

We have noted the chronic lack of infrastructure finance data in terms of correctly identified statistics, investment patterns, debt ratings, debt and equity performance, liquidity, and other attributes that help to define markets and reduce the risk of engaging with them. A 2016 joint initiative on the part of the Monetary Authority of Singapore (MAS), the French business school EDHEC, and the French investment bank Natixis aimed to launch a $14 million research unit staffed by 10 economists and statisticians mandated to create a comprehensive infrastructure financing dataset by 2021. This dataset could then be used for benchmarking infrastructure financings around the world, improve

---

3   Including 144A bonds as well as Section 4(a)(2) and Regulation D private placements.

4   The US National Association of Securities Dealers (NASD) introduced TRACE (Trade Reporting and Compliance Engine) in July 2002 in an effort to increase price transparency in the US corporate debt market. The system captures and disseminates consolidated information on secondary market transactions in publicly traded TRACE-eligible securities (investment grade, high yield, and convertible corporate debt), representing all over-the-counter market activity in these bonds. See http://www.finra.org/industry/trace/corporate-bond-data#sthash. P4m5q0An.dpuf

institutional investors' understanding of the asset class, and improve the management of risks.

This initiative's ultimate objective is creating tradable products such as a new generation of infrastructure-based collateralized debt obligations (CDOs). Unlike the last wave of subprime mortgage-backed CDOs in the mid-2000s, these assets would be transparent, tradable, and fully understood by institutional investors. This venture could put Singapore at the center of the action in terms of origination and trading of a new global asset class with acceptable liquidity properties.

The first benchmark, focused only on OECD infrastructure financing, was due to be published at the end of 2016. Without trading data, the initiative's success will depend entirely on cooperation from institutional investors, banks, and other investors. The dataset reportedly contains 500 infrastructure debt and equity issues over 25 years, with plans to eventually expand to 2,000 entities.[5]

15.6 Lack of Viable Infrastructure Projects

So far, all of the impediments to increasing the flow of infrastructure debt capital from the investment-grade bond market have not presented a serious blockage to market expansion because of the dearth of viable projects in need of financing. Moreover, a wave of refinancing activity since the 2007–2008 global financial crisis has further tempered any financial supply issues because interest rates have plummeted. From 2010 through 2015, about one-fourth of total new project finance debt issuance involved refinancing of existing on-line projects.

Already-operating or brownfield projects located in OECD countries with strong equity sponsorship (especially projects that are government-related) and long-term offtake contracts with high-quality counterparties currently have no trouble finding financing. In fact, most such deals are oversubscribed.

At the other end of the spectrum, projects that struggle to find economically-priced debt and are effectively closed out of the global financial markets are located mainly in lower-rated, non-investment-grade

---

5   http://www.straitstimes.com/business/economy/mas-in-joint-bid-to-set-up-new-
investment-database

countries where sovereign risk looms large, predominantly in Latin America and Africa. This situation is highly unfortunate because the properly executed and financed development of power, water, and telecommunications infrastructure could dramatically accelerate economic growth and living standards in such countries.[6]

For perspective, based on the Standard & Poor's rated sovereign universe as of December 2015, roughly two thirds of the 193 UN member countries were rated below investment grade or not rated at all (and thus implicitly non-investment grade). Approximately 40% of the world's current population lives in these 124 countries, which in the aggregate generated only an estimated one quarter of world GDP in 2015.

No amount of bond market innovation or contractual/legal structuring, however, can effectively mitigate or compensate for the poor governance, rampant corruption, and expropriation risk that afflicts such countries. Even off-shore cash lock-boxes and international arbitration panels provide little help, because the underlying weaknesses are mainly political and social in nature. Investor memories of the Argentine and Venezuelan project bond defaults some 10 to 15 years ago have yet to fade. At worst, poorly conceived, governed, and executed infrastructure projects that fail to generate the economic capacity to service the contractual financing can leave countries and their citizens worse off even if the financing providers are made whole.

Much more subtle are local rules governing infrastructure investments that effectively discriminate against foreign investments which compete with local interests.

A good example is India's Securitisation and Reconstruction of Financial Assets and Enforcement of Security Interest Act of 2002 (Sarfaesi), which provides access to non-performing secured assets without the intervention of Indian courts by following a streamlined alternative procedure. Given India's inefficient legal system, Sarfaesi

---

6   An interesting exception is a bond issue for the 2015 $522 million "Rutas de Lima" toll road infrastructure project in Peru. This example shows that a well-structured PPP initiative in a developing country with impressive public policy credentials can open up new, cost-effective channels of financing. For background, see http://www.bnamericas.com/en/news/infrastructure/rutas-de-lima-in-record-us522mn-bond-issue

was designed to encourage investments, including in infrastructure, by cutting legal risk in the event of default. Foreign creditors, however, are not classed as secured lenders under the Act and, unlike their Indian competitors and co-financiers, could not avail themselves of Sarfaesi's streamlined provisions (notwithstanding *pari passu* and inter-creditor agreements). Under such circumstances, foreign lenders end up at the mercy of lengthy and uncertain Indian court proceedings.

Such rules, which seem clearly protectionist and provide a potentially decisive advantage to domestic lenders, are unlikely to promote the Indian market for project investment. Given India's size and importance, this regulation could extract a high cost in terms of the country's future infrastructure development.

16. Some Solutions

Infrastructure projects that meet sound commercial standards in terms of the returns and risks discussed in this study — including the sovereign dimensions — tend to find acceptable financing in the global debt markets. More such financing will become available as those markets become more capable of absorbing this asset class.

Projects that cannot meet these standards must rely on public finance and varying domestic or external guarantee structures. In many cases, this means explicit or implicit subsidies, or an assessment that the *social* returns and risks paint a significantly more favorable picture than purely *market-driven* assessments of the returns and risks. Such an outcome may be reasonable, but it places the burden of financing back on the public sector. The end objective is to shift the funding to the private sector in a sensible way whilst generating excess gains that the broader community of infrastructure stakeholders can share.

Given bank lending's already dominant role, the greatest potential arguably lies in expanding the universe of infrastructure projects that can secure financing in the investment-grade bond market. A number of approaches to this end seem possible.

First, because investment-grade ratings would by definition be a prerequisite for projects to win broad-gauge bond market financing, credit enhancement techniques — such as interest and principal guarantees provided by bond insurers — offer one means of elevating some lower-rated high-yield international projects into the low end of the BBB ratings category.

If a higher-rated corporate sponsor is involved, a contingent financial guarantee might be possible. As noted, certain supranational agencies (e.g., the European Investment Bank) have begun to develop financing programs to bolster the credit ratings and institutional investor demand for targeted project finance bonds.

Possible credit enhancements suggest the key role that various multilateral development banks could play to unlock market-based financing for projects in the world's poorest and in some cases most incompetently run countries. Because the problem of capital market access is heavily political, supranational financial institutions seem uniquely qualified to exert influence on member states and address the underlying governance issues that hold back such projects.

The World Bank, founded in 1944 as the International Bank for Reconstruction and Development to help finance post-war recovery, soon morphed into a key institution with the ultimate goal of eradicating world poverty. So far, the track record of this institution and its regional counterparts in reaching that overarching objective is decidedly mixed if the objective is a reduction in global poverty.

In 2014, a significant portion of the World Bank's lending went to member countries that were already rated investment grade, with access to both developed local financial markets as well as the international bond markets. The Asia Pacific region, in particular, has absorbed a disproportionate amount of concessional credit from the multilateral lenders, on a scale largely inconsistent with the region's already impressive development and growth performance.

To be sure, the World Bank and the other multilateral development banks have provided loans (typically early-stage) mainly to projects located in their member countries. Such lending has been limited in scope (typically 3% of total project debt) and has ranked super-senior in debt-service priority, based on these institutions' preferred creditor status.

The halo effect from such project lending, however, appears to have been an insufficient catalyst to spur greater infrastructure development in poor regions, or even to preclude outright defaults on some of the projects bearing a supranational stamp of approval.

From an institutional investor's perspective, having the World Bank or its cohorts able to exit and be paid off first is not as much of a "credit positive" as, for example, having the same type of capital invested in much greater volume on a junior basis. The latter exemplifies how the aforementioned EC/EIB credit enhancement program would work (i.e., a subordinated tranche of capital). Such junior debt or equity capital provided by the supranational agency would still be backed by the pledged capital from the member country where a particular project is located, helping to mitigate the lending institution's risk of loss.

Although such a credit enhancement program would require a re-working of the various multilateral development banks' stated mandates, as well as a reallocation of resources within these institutions, the potential benefits apparently justify the effort. Moreover, by having the supranational agencies exert a greater influence on specific projects through a more significant role in the capital structure, better governance standards should follow. For its part, the World Bank seems ideally positioned to invent clever enhancements that would kick infrastructure projects on the margin into the low investment-grade category and open up large, previously off-limits asset pools for such projects.

The World Bank recently created a Global Infrastructure Facility platform to encourage the sharing of best practices in PPP project development across the developing world. Having more of an equity-style ownership role in specific project financings would give supranational agencies much more leverage to ensure that these projects pursue the best international standards. Moreover, the strong support of an AAA-rated supranational agency might be sufficient to pierce the sovereign ceiling of lower-rated countries and achieve investment-grade ratings for specific projects.

The World Bank's new rival is the China-dominated, 21-country, $100 billion Asian Infrastructure Investment Bank (AIIB). It is too early to tell whether this organization will follow the same pattern as the World Bank in focusing excessively on infrastructure projects in those countries that already stand the best chances of fending for themselves in world capital markets.

Individual OECD governments might also consider repurposing their sovereign credit agencies — which until now have been involved in infrastructure project loans on a limited, senior basis alongside multilateral and commercial bank lenders — to play a similar junior capital role in promoting specific projects in targeted countries. Such repurposing would move these agencies away from their historically narrow focus on specific trade-related initiatives and toward providing broader support for economic development in these nations' key trading partners.

Additionally, the pool of available sovereign-related capital could be augmented in certain countries using re-channeled bilateral aid volumes from consumption to infrastructure development, as well as redirected investment capital from sovereign wealth funds interested in playing a catalytic role in global infrastructure.

The same infusion of best practices and good governance would likely follow if a government institution such as the US' Private Export Funding Corporation, Export Development Canada, or Germany's KfW Development Bank assumed a more prominent creditor (or even equity) role in infrastructure projects for developing countries, unlike the minimal, supplementary lending role these agencies have played in the past.

Some countries have considered national "infrastructure banks" that raise capital at or near sovereign rates or provide guarantees at below-market rates. There have been multiple calls for the creation of an infrastructure bank in the US — especially during the 2016 election cycle, and other countries have already deployed such institutions. In some circumstances, these special structures can reduce project costs by reducing the perceived risk for lenders and investors because they offer collateral, stronger creditor rights, and the like. They can also bring greater technical expertise to an infrastructure project and help shield it (for better or for worse) from the whims of local politics.

An infrastructure bank, however, could also turn out to be a cost-increasing end-run around local politics and would surely have higher financing costs than using straight sovereign debt in financing the same infrastructure. On the other hand, an infrastructure bank's special debt class would likely not be considered part of a country's "national debt" and might avoid "debt ceiling" political machinations.

Given the political realities, however, comingling private and public finance often does not end well — for instance, Fannie Mae and Freddie Mac in the US or the Economic Development Bank in Puerto Rico. The burden falls squarely on infrastructure bank advocates to make a convincing case that the benefits exceed the costs compared to market-based solutions.

Borrowing ideas from other areas of capital-intensive financing could also be productive. Consider the Cape Town Convention, which covers international financing of commercial aircraft and aircraft engines (2001), railroad equipment (2007), and aerospace assets (2012). It created international standards for registration of contracts of sale (including dedicated registration agencies), security interests (liens), leases and conditional sales contracts, and various legal remedies for default in financing agreements, including repossession and alignment with signatory countries' bankruptcy laws. Its treaty came into force in 2004 and has been ratified by 57 countries.

By creating a common platform to secure lender rights, the Cape Town Convention moves key risks for registered equipment outside a nation's sovereign domain and assures contracts' enforceability, yielding common gains for signatory countries, air and land transport firms, lenders, and ultimately consumers.[1] It has been highly successful in extracting gains for a broad range of stakeholders. Adapting this kind of innovation to infrastructure finance may be well worth considering.

---

1   See Saunders, Srinivasan, Walter and Wool (1999).

References

[n.a.], 2014. "A Long and Winding Road". *The Economist*, 22 March 2014, http://www.economist.com/news/finance-and-economics/21599394-world-needs-more-infrastructure-how-will-it-pay-it-long-and-windin

Bhattacharya, Amar, Jeremy Oppenheim, and Nicholas Stern. 2015. "Driving Sustainable Development through Better Infrastructure". Working Paper 91. The Brookings Institution.

Binmore, Ken, and Paul Klemperer. 2002. "The Biggest Auction Ever: The Sale of the British 3G Telecom Licences". *Economic Journal* 112 (478): C74–C96. http://dx.doi.org/10.1111/1468-0297.00020

Caves, Richard E. 1971. "International Corporations: The Industrial Economics of Foreign Investment". *Economica* 38 (149): 1–27, http://dx.doi.org/10.2307/2551748

Chiang, Yao-Min, Yiming Qian, and Ann E. Sherman. 2010. "Endogenous Entry and Partial Adjustment in IPO Auctions: Are Institutional Investors Better Informed?" *Review of Financial Studies* 23 (3): 1200–230. http://dx.doi.org/10.1093/rfs/hhp066

Dupire, Marion, Freddy Van den Spiegel, and Katia Villaseca Palomeque. 2015. "Regulating Long Term Finance in the European Union: Challenges and Opportunities". Vlerick Business School, *Vlerick Policy Paper Series* No. 3, August 2015.

Cournot, Augustin. 1838/1995. *Researches into the Mathematical Principles of the Theory of Wealth Recherches Sur Les Principes Mathématiques De La Théorie Des Richesses [Recherches Sur Les Principes Mathématiques De La Théorie Des Richesses]*. Translated by Nathaniel T. Bacon. Mountain Center, CA: James and Gordon. Original edition, Paris: L. Hachette.

Finnerty, J.D. 2013. *Project Financing: Asset-Based Financial Engineering*. New York: John Wiley & Sons.

Funk, Weill, and Hodes. 2014. *Institutional Real Estate Allocations Monitor*. New York: Hodes Weill Associates.

Ghemawat, Pankaj. 2001. "Distance Still Matters: The Hard Reality of Global Expansion". *Harvard Business Review* 79 (8): 137–47.

Ghemawat, Pankaj, and Steven A. Altman. 2014. "DHL Global Connectedness Index 2014", http://www.dhl.com/en/about_us/logistics_insights/studies_research/global_connectedness_index/global_connectedness_index.html

Ghemawat, Pankaj, and Thomas M. Hout. 2016. "Globalization, Capabilities, and Distance: Theory and a Case Study (of China)". In *Oxford Handbook of Dynamic Capabilities*, edited by David J. Teece. Oxford: Oxford University Press. http://dx.doi.org/10.1093/oxfordhb/9780199678914.013.009

Hanouz, Margareta Drzeniek, Thierry Geiger, and Sean Doherty, eds. 2014. *The Global Enabling Trade Report 2014*. Geneva: World Economic Forum, http://www3.weforum.org/docs/WEF_GlobalEnablingTrade_Report_2014.pdf

Hausman, William J., Peter Hertner, and Mira Wilkins. 2008. *Global Electrification: Multinational Enterprise and International Finance in the History of Light and Power, 1878–2007*. Cambridge: Cambridge University Press.

Head, Keith, and Thierry Mayer. 2014. "Gravity Equations: Workhorse, Toolkit, and Cookbook". In *Handbook of International Economics*, edited by Gita Gopinath, Elhanan Helpman, and Kenneth S. Rogoff, Vol. 4, pp. 131–95. http://dx.doi.org/10.1016/B978-0-444-54314-1.00003-3

Hill, Raymond, and L.G. Thomas III. 2005. "Moths to a Flame: Social Proof, Reputation, and Status in the Overseas Electricity Bubble". Working paper. Emory University, Goizueta Business School, May 2005, http://goizueta.emory.edu/profiles/documents/publications_working_papers/thomas/mothstoaflame.pdf

Hout, Thomas, and Pankaj Ghemawat. 2010. "China vs. the World: Whose Technology Is It?" *Harvard Business Review* 88 (12): 94–103.

Hout, Thomas, and David Michael. 2014. "A Chinese Approach to Management". *Harvard Business Review* 92 (9): 103–07.

Kahale, Özgür Can. 2011. "Project Finance and the Relevant Human Rights", in *Global Project Finance, Human Rights and Sustainable Development*, by Sheldon Leader and David Ong (New York: Cambridge University Press), pp. 37-76.

Klemperer, Paul. 2002a. "How (Not) To Run Auctions: The European 3G Telecom Auctions". *European Economic Review* 46 (4–5): 829–45. http://dx.doi.org/10.1016/S0014-2921(01)00218-5

—. 2002b. "What Really Matters in Auction Design". *Journal of Economic Perspectives* 16 (1): 169–89. http://dx.doi.org/10.1257/0895330027166

Mayer, Thierry, and Soledad Zignago. *Geodist Dataset*. CEPII, December 12, 2011, http://www.cepii.fr/CEPII/fr/bdd_modele/download.asp?id=6

McKinsey Global Institute, Richard Dobbs, Herbert Pohl, Diaan-Yi Lin, Jan Mischke, Nicklas Garemo, Jimmy Hexter, Stefan Matzinger, Robert Palter, and Rushad Nanavatty. January 2013. *Infrastructure Productivity: How to Save $1 Trillion a Year*. New York: McKinsey Global Institute, http://www.mckinsey.com/insights/engineering_construction/infrastructure_productivity

Meltzer, Joshua P. 2015. "Financing Sustainable Infrastructure". The Brookings Institution, https://www.brookings.edu/wp-content/uploads/2016/08/global_20160818_financing_sustainable_infrastructure.pdf

Nixon, Ron. 2015. "Obama's 'Power Africa' Project Is Off to a Sputtering Start". *New York Times*, 21 July.

Nomura Securities. 2014. Private presentation.

Paddock, Richard C. 2016. "Justice Department Rejects Account of How Malaysia's Leader Acquired Millions", *New York Times*, 22 July.

Saunders, Anthony, Anand Srinivasan, Ingo Walter, and Jeffrey Wool. 1999. "Proposed Unidroit Convention on International Interests in Mobile Equipment". *University of Pennsylvania Journal of International Economic Law* (Fall): 1–44.

Sherman, Ann E. 2005. "Global Trends in IPO Methods: Book Building versus Auctions with Endogenous Entry". *Journal of Financial Economics* 78 (3): 615–49. http://dx.doi.org/10.1016/j.jfineco.2004.09.005

Sirri, Erik R. 2014. *Report on Secondary Market Trading in the Municipal Securities Market*. Municipal Securities Rulemaking Board, http://www.msrb.org/msrb1/pdfs/MSRB-Report-on-Secondary-Market-Trading-in-the-Municipal-Securities-Market.pdf

Smith, Roy C., Ingo Walter and Gayle DeLong. 2012. *Global Banking*, 3rd edition. New York: Oxford University Press. Chapter 3: Asset-Related and Project Financing. http://dx.doi.org/10.1093/acprof:oso/9780195335934.001.0001

Sutton, John. 2012. *Competing in Capabilities: The Globalization Process*, Clarendon Lectures in Economics. Oxford: Oxford University Press. http://dx.doi.org/10.1093/acprof:oso/9780199274536.001.0001

Tice, Paul, and Ingo Walter. 2014. *BlackRock Infrastructure Finance*. Fontainebleau, Insead, and Brussels, European Case Clearing House.

Transparency International. 2014. "The Corruption Perceptions Index 2014." https://www.transparency.org

Tulacz, Gary J. 2013. "The Top 250 International Contractors". *ENR: Engineering News-Record* 271 (8): 2–2.

UNCTAD. 2014. UNCTAD Surveys of Infrastructure Regulators and Competition Authorities. Geneva: United Nations Conference on Trade and Development, http://unctad.org/en/pages/PublicationWebflyer.aspx?publicationid=547

Whitehead, Charles K. 2011. "The Volcker Rule and Evolving Financial Markets". *Harvard Business Law Review* 1: 11–19.

World Bank. 2015. *World Development Indicators*. Washington, DC: World Bank, http://data.worldbank.org/products/wdi

World Economic Forum. 2014. *Infrastructure Investment Policy Blueprint*. Geneva: WEF.

Contributors

Working Group on Infrastructure Finance
Stern School of Business, New York University

Pankaj Ghemawat, Professor of Management

Joel Hasbrouck, Professor of Finance

Peter Henry, Professor of Economics

Michael Posner, Professor of Business and Society

Paul Romer, Professor of Economics

Michael Spence, Professor of Economics

Paul Tice, Executive in Residence

Stijn Van Nieuwerburgh, Professor of Finance

Ingo Walter, Professor Emeritus of Finance

Tensie Whelan, Professor of Business and Society

Lawrence White, Professor of Economics

David Yermack, Professor of Finance

Contributors' Bios

Pankaj Ghemawat joined New York University Stern School of Business in September 2014 as Global Professor of Management and Strategy in Stern's Management & Organizations Department. Professor Ghemawat has been appointed by Stern to lead the new Center for the Globalization of Education and Management, to drive scholarship and pedagogy on the business implications of globalization. He is also the Anselmo Rubiralta Professor of Global Strategy at IESE Business School. Pankaj has written five books and more than 100 research articles and case studies on global business strategy and is one of the world's best-selling authors of teaching cases. He also compiles an annual globalization index that looks at the connectivity of more than 130 countries with the rest of the world in terms of trade, capital, information and people flows.

Pankaj is a fellow of the Academy of International Business and of the Strategic Management Society. A recent book, *World 3.0* (2011, Harvard Business Review Press), re-examines beliefs about markets and globalization, praising market integration whilst addressing its potential negative ramifications against the goal of increasing prosperity. *World 3.0* won the 50 Thinkers Book Award for the best business book published in 2010–2011, the Axiom Business Book Gold Award in the International Business/Globalization category and the IESE Alumni Research Excellence Award. In August 2014 Pankaj received the Eminent Scholar award of the International Management Division of the Academy of Management.

From 1983 to 2008, Pankaj was on the faculty of Harvard Business School, becoming the youngest person in the school's history to be appointed a full professor, in 1991. He was also the youngest "guru" included in the guide to the greatest management thinkers of all time, published in 2008 by *The Economist*. Since 2006, he has been on the faculty of IESE.

Pankaj earned both his B.S. in Applied Mathematics and his PhD in Business Economics from Harvard University.

Joel Hasbrouck is the Kenneth G. Langone Professor of Business Administration and Professor of Finance at the Stern School of Business, NYU. His research focuses on the analysis, design and regulation of securities trading mechanisms (market microstructure). He is the author of *Empirical Market Microstructure* (Oxford, 2006) and numerous articles. Joel is presently an Advisory Editor of the *Journal of Financial Markets*, and an Associate Editor of the *Journal of Financial Econometrics*, the *Journal of Financial Intermediation*, and a former editor of the *Review of Financial Studies*.

He holds MA and PhD degrees from the University of Pennsylvania and a BS in Chemistry from Haverford College.

Peter Blair Henry is the Dean of New York University's Stern School of Business and a former Professor of International Economics at Stanford University. He is also the author of *Turnaround: Third World Lessons for First World Growth* (Basic Books, 2013). In 2008, Peter led Barack Obama's Presidential Transition Team in its review of international lending agencies such as the IMF and World Bank. A member of the Federal Reserve Bank of New York's Economic Advisory Panel and a member of the boards of the National Bureau of Economic Research (NBER), the Council on Foreign Relations, Citi, and General Electric, in 2015, Peter was awarded the Foreign Policy Association Medal, the highest honor bestowed by the organization. Peter received his PhD in Economics from MIT and Bachelor's degrees from Oxford University, where he was a Rhodes Scholar, and the University of North Carolina, where he was a Morehead Scholar and a finalist in the 1991 campus-wide slam dunk competition. Born in Jamaica, Peter became a US citizen in 1986. He lives in New York City with his wife of 20 years and their four sons.

Michael H. Posner is the Jerome Kohlberg Professor of Ethics and Finance and a Professor of Business and Society at NYU's Stern School of Business, where he is working to launch the first-ever center on business and human rights at a business school. Prior to joining NYU Stern, Michael served from 2009 to 2013 in the Obama Administration as Assistant Secretary of State for the Bureau of Democracy, Human Rights and Labor at the State Department. From 1978 to 2009, he led Human Rights First, a New York-based human rights advocacy organization.

Michael is recognized as a leader and expert in advancing a rights-based approach to national security, challenging the practice of torture, combating discrimination, and promoting refugee protection. He is a frequent public commentator on these issues, and has testified dozens of times before the US Congress. As Assistant Secretary, Michael traveled extensively, representing the US Government to foreign officials and representatives of civil society in countries of strategic importance to the US, including China, Russia, Egypt, Burma, Bahrain, Nigeria, Afghanistan, and Pakistan, among many others.

Throughout his career, Michael has been a prominent voice in support of human rights protections in global business operations in the manufacturing supply chain, the extractives industry, and the information and communications technology sector. As a member of the White House Apparel Industry Partnership Task Force in the mid-'90s, he helped found the Fair Labor Association (FLA), an organization that brings together corporations, local leaders, universities, and NGOs to promote corporate accountability for working conditions in the apparel industry. He was a founding member of the Global Network Initiative, a multi-stakeholder initiative aimed at promoting free expression and privacy rights on the Internet, and has spoken widely on the issue of Internet freedom. Michael spearheaded the US Government's efforts to enhance the effectiveness of the Voluntary Principles on Security and Human Rights, which works to improve human rights around oil, gas, and mining operations.

Michael played a key role in proposing and campaigning for the first US law providing for political asylum, which became part of the Refugee Act of 1980, as well as the Torture Victim Protection Act, which was adopted in 1992. In 1998, he led the Human Rights First delegation to the Rome conference at which the statute of the International Criminal Court (ICC) was adopted.

Before joining Human Rights First, Michael was a lawyer with Sonnenschein, Nath & Rosenthal in Chicago. He lectured at Yale Law School from 1981 to 1984, and again in 2009, when he taught with former Dean Harold Koh. He was a visiting lecturer at Columbia University Law School from 1984 to 2008. A member of the California Bar and the Illinois Bar, he received his J.D. from the University of California, Berkeley Law School (Boalt Hall) in 1975, and a BA with distinction and honors in History from the University of Michigan in 1972.

Paul Romer is a University Professor at NYU and director of its Marron Institute of Urban Management. His work now focuses on urbanization because better urban policy offers the best chance for speeding up growth in the developing world.

Paul is currently on leave as Chief Economist at the World Bank. Before coming to NYU. He taught at Stanford, and while there, started Aplia, an education technology company. In 2002, he received the Recktenwald Prize for work on the economics of ideas and the drivers of economic growth.

Paul earned a B.S. in Mathematics and a PhD in Economics from the University of Chicago.

Michael Spence is Professor of Economics at the Stern School at NYU, Professor Emeritus of Management in the Graduate School of Business at Stanford University, a Senior Fellow of the Hoover Institution at Stanford.

Michael received the Nobel Prize in Economic Sciences in 2001, and the John Bates Clark Medal in 1982, for work on markets with asymmetrical information. He is the author of the book, *The Next Convergence: The Future of Economic Growth in a Multispeed World* (Ferrar, Straus and Giroux, 2011).

He served as dean of the Stanford Business School from 1990 to 1999. As dean, he oversaw the finances, organization, and educational policies of the school. Michael currently serves on the board of Mercadolibre, and a number of private companies. He is a member of the board of the Stanford Management Company, and the International Chamber of Commerce Research Foundation. He is a Senior Advisor to Oak Hill Investment Management, and a consultant to PIMCO. He is the chairman of the academic board of the Fung Global Institute, based in Hong Kong. He recently became a member of the Advisory Board of the School of Economics and Management of Tsinghua University.

Michael chaired the Independent Commission on Growth and Development (active from 2006 to 2010) dealing with growth in developing countries.

Paul Tice is a Senior Managing Director and Head of the Energy Capital Group in the Asset Management division of US Capital Advisors LLC, an energy-focused financial services boutique. Prior to joining USCA in 2015, he worked at BlackRock, where he was the Head of private energy investments for the firm's Credit platform and Americas Fixed Income business, while also serving as the Lead Portfolio Manager for the Energy Strategy book within BlackRock's R3 Fund.

Prior to joining BlackRock in 2009, Paul was the Chief Operating Officer, Co-Chief Investment Officer and a Senior Partner of R3 Capital Management, a multi-strategy, credit-focused hedge fund manager that was spun out of Lehman Brothers in May 2008 and subsequently acquired by BlackRock in April 2009.

Prior to R3, Paul worked for a total of 14 years at Lehman Brothers (2002–2008, 1989–1997) in a variety of roles, most recently as a Managing Director in the firm's Global Principal Strategies (GPS) division, an internal, credit-focused proprietary fund that was formed in June 2006 and spun out in May 2008. While at GPS, Paul supervised the fund's investments in the energy and power sector, while also managing the overall GPS research effort and approving all private equity and longer-term investments by the fund.

Prior to joining the GPS group in 2006, Paul spent 17 years in sell-side credit research, both at Lehman Brothers and Deutsche Bank/Bankers Trust (1997–2002), where he mainly covered the energy sector, both as a senior analyst and a producing manager.

Paul has covered the energy sector since 1995 and was one of the top-ranked Investment Grade Energy analysts over 1995–2006. In 2006 and 1998, he was the #1 ranked Investment Grade Energy analyst on Institutional Investor's All-America Fixed Income Research Team. Prior to originally joining Lehman Brothers in 1989, he was a senior financial analyst at JPMorgan Chase.

Paul has previously served on the Board of Directors for Lightfoot Capital Partners GP LLC and Richland-Stryker Investment LLC, two investment portfolio companies of the R3 Fund.

He earned a BA degree in English, *magna cum laude*, from Columbia University in 1983, and an MBA degree in Finance from the Leonard N. Stern School of Business at New York University in 1988. He is a member of Phi Beta Kappa.

Paul is currently Executive-in-Residence at the Leonard N. Stern School of Business at New York University, where he is a guest lecturer, panel speaker and research contributor, and periodically writes Op-Ed pieces on energy- and finance-related topics in *The Wall Street Journal* and other news media.

Stijn Van Nieuwerburgh is the David S. Loeb Professor of Finance and the Director of the Center for Real Estate Finance Research at New York University Leonard N. Stern School of Business, which he joined in 2003.

Stijn's research lies in the intersection of housing, asset pricing, and macroeconomics. One strand of his work studies how financial market liberalization in the mortgage market relaxed households' down payment constraints, and how that affected the macro-economy, and the prices of stocks and bonds. In this area, he has also worked on regional housing prices and on household's mortgage choice. He currently studies real estate price formation, and the impact of foreign buyers on the market.

He has published articles in a range of journals including the *Journal of Political Economy, American Economic Review, Econometrica, Review of Economic Studies, Journal of Finance, Review of Financial Studies, Journal of Financial Economics*, and the *Journal of Monetary Economics*, among other journals. He is Editor at the Review of Financial Studies. He is a Faculty Research Associate at the National Bureau of Economic Research and at the Center for European Policy Research.

Stijn has served as an advisor to the Norwegian Minister of Finance, and has been a visiting scholar at to the Central Bank of Belgium, the New York and Minneapolis Federal Reserve Banks, the Swedish House of Finance, the International Center for Housing Risk, and has contributed to the World Economic Forum project on real estate price dynamics.

He earned his PhD in Economics and MA in Financial Mathematics at Stanford University and his BA degree in Economics at the University of Ghent in Belgium.

Ingo Walter is Seymour Milstein Professor Emeritus of Finance, Corporate Governance and Ethics at the Stern School of Business, New York University.

From 1971 to 1979 he was Vice Dean for Academic Affairs and subsequently served a number of terms as Chair of International Business and Chair of Finance. He served as Director of the New York University Salomon Center for the Study of Financial Institutions (1990 -2003) and Director of the Stern Global Business Institute (2003-2006). He was Vice Dean of the Faculty of the Stern School from 2008 to 2012.

Ingo has had visiting professorial appointments at the Free University of Berlin, University of Mannheim, University of Zurich, University of Basel, the Institute for Southeast Asian Studies in Singapore, IESE in Spain, NYU Abu Dhabi, the University of Western Australia and various other academic and research institutions. He also held a joint appointment as Professor of International Management at INSEAD from 1986 to 2005 and remains a visiting professor there.

His current areas of academic activity include international financial intermediation and banking. He has published papers in most of the professional journals in these fields and has authored or coauthored some two dozen books and monographs, and has served as a consultant to various corporations, banks, government agencies and international institutions.

Ingo received his AB *summa cum laude* and MS degrees from Lehigh University and his PhD degree from NYU, and has been on the faculty at NYU since 1970.

Tensie Whelan is the Director of NYU Stern School of Business's Center for Sustainable Business, where she is bringing her 25 years of experience working on local, national and international environmental and sustainability issues to engage businesses in proactive and innovative mainstreaming of sustainability.

As President of the Rainforest Alliance, Tansie built the organization from a $4.5 million to $50 million budget, transforming the engagement of business with sustainability, recruiting 5,000 companies in more than 60 countries to work with Rainforest Alliance.

Her previous work included serving as Executive Director of the New York League of Conservation Voters, Vice President of the National Audubon Society, Managing Editor of *Ambio*, a journal of the Swedish Academy of Sciences, and a journalist in Latin America.

Tensie has been recognized by Ethisphere as one of the 100 Most Influential People in Business Ethics, was the Citi Fellow in Leadership and Ethics at NYU Stern in 2015 and has served on corporate advisory boards such as the Unilever Sustainable Sourcing Advisory Board and the Nespresso Innovation Fund Advisory Board.

Lawrence J. White is the Robert Kavesh Professor of Economics at New York University's Stern School of Business and Deputy Chair of the Economics Department at Stern. During 1986–1989 he was on leave to serve as Board Member, Federal Home Loan Bank Board, in which capacity he also served as Board Member for Freddie Mac; and during 1982–1983 he was on leave to serve as Director of the Economic Policy Office, Antitrust Division, US Department of Justice. He is the General

Editor of *The Review of Industrial Organization* and formerly Secretary-Treasurer of the Western Economic Association International.

Larry received his BA from Harvard University (1964), his M.Sc. from the London School of (1965), and his PhD from Harvard University (1969).

He is the author of *The Automobile Industry Since 1945* (1971); *Industrial Concentration and Economic Power in Pakistan* (1974); *Reforming Regulation: Processes and Problems* (1981); *The Regulation of Air Pollutant Emissions from Motor Vehicles* (1982); *The Public Library in the 1980s: The Problems of Choice* (1983); *International Trade in Ocean Shipping Services: The US and the World* (1988); *The S&L Debacle: Public Policy Lessons for Bank and Thrift Regulation* (1991); and articles in leading economics, finance, and law journals. He is the co-author (with V.V. Acharya, M. Richardson, and S. Van Nieuwerburgh) of *Guaranteed to Fail: Fannie Mae, Freddie Mac, and the Debacle of Mortgage Finance*, Princeton University Press, 2011.

Larry is editor or coeditor of twelve volumes: *Deregulation of the Banking and Securities Industries* (1979); *Mergers and Acquisitions: Current Problems in Perspective* (1982); *Technology and the Regulation of Financial Markets: Securities, Futures, and Banking* (1986); *Private Antitrust Litigation: New Evidence, New Learning* (1988); *The Antitrust Revolution* (1989); *Bank Management and Regulation* (1992); *Structural Change in Banking* (1993); *The Antitrust Revolution: The Role of Economics* (6 editions). He was the North American Editor of *The Journal of Industrial Economics*, 1984–1987 and 1990–1995.

Larry served on the Senior Staff of the President's Council of Economic Advisers during 1978–1979, and he was Chairman of the Stern School's Department of Economics from 1990 to 1995.

David L. Yermack is the Albert Fingerhut Professor of Finance and Business Transformation and Chairman of the Finance Department at New York University's Stern School of Business, where he has been a member of the faculty since 1994. He is also an Adjunct Professor of Law at the New York University School of Law, Director of the NYU Pollack Center for Law and Business, and a Research Associate of the National Bureau of Economic Research law and economics program.

At NYU David teaches a joint MBA-JD course, *Restructuring Firms and Industries*, as well as doctoral level courses on corporate governance, corporate restructuring, and executive compensation. In 2014 he began teaching the first course at a major university on digital currencies and blockchains in the financial services industry.

David has published more than 25 papers in peer-reviewed academic journals, including some of the most cited papers in the fields of executive compensation and corporate governance. He has also written papers on such diverse topics as options in baseball player contracts, incentive compensation for clergymen, tobacco litigation, fraudulent charitable contributions, CEOs' mansions, the governance of art museums, and Michelle Obama's impact on the fashion industry.

David was awarded AB (1985), MBA (1991), JD (1991), AM (1993) and PhD (1994) degrees, all from Harvard University. He is on the editorial boards of five leading finance journals and was elected in 2008 as an academic member of the board of directors of the Financial Management Association. David has been appointed a visiting professor at 15 international universities, a visiting scholar at the Federal Reserve Banks of New York and Philadelphia, and has given invited research seminars at more than 100 universities and institutes worldwide. David has work experience in management consulting, law, and financial journalism.

This book need not end here...

At Open Book Publishers, we are changing the nature of the traditional academic book. The title you have just read will not be left on a library shelf, but will be accessed online by hundreds of readers each month across the globe. OBP publishes only the best academic work: each title passes through a rigorous peer-review process. We make all our books free to read online so that students, researchers and members of the public who can't afford a printed edition will have access to the same ideas.

This book and additional content is available at:
http://www.openbookpublishers.com/isbn/9781783742936

Customize

Personalize your copy of this book or design new books using OBP and third-party material. Take chapters or whole books from our published list and make a special edition, a new anthology or an illuminating coursepack. Each customized edition will be produced as a paperback and a downloadable PDF. Find out more at:

http://www.openbookpublishers.com/section/59/1

Donate

If you enjoyed this book, and feel that research like this should be available to all readers, regardless of their income, please think about donating to us. We do not operate for profit and all donations, as with all other revenue we generate, will be used to finance new Open Access publications.

http://www.openbookpublishers.com/section/13/1/support-us

Like Open Book Publishers

Follow @OpenBookPublish

Read more at the Open Book Publishers BLOG

You may also be interested in:

The Universal Declaration of Human Rights in the 21st Century
Edited by Gordon Brown

https://www.openbookpublishers.com/product/467

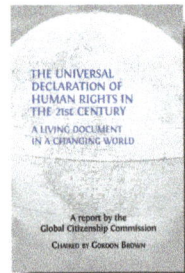

Democracy and Power
The Delhi Lectures
Noam Chomsky. Introduction by Jean Drèze

https://www.openbookpublishers.com/product/300

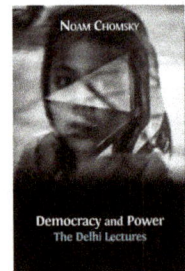

Peace and Democratic Society
Edited by Amartya Sen

http://www.openbookpublishers.com/product/78

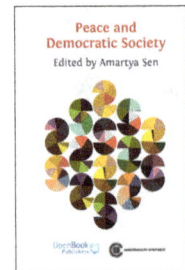

www.ingramcontent.com/pod-product-compliance
Lightning Source LLC
Chambersburg PA
CBHW061333220326
41599CB00026B/5156